Power Of Believing

By
Karim Hajee

"Every day, think as you wake up, today I am fortunate to be alive, I have a precious human life, I am not going to waste it. I am going to use all my energies to develop myself, to expand my heart out to others; to achieve enlightenment for the benefit of all beings. I am going to have kind thoughts towards others, I am not going to get angry or think badly about others. I am going to benefit others as much as I can."

- The Dalai Lama

Power Of Believing

Second Edition - 2006
©Karim Hajee
All Rights Reserved
ISBN: 0-9738981-0-0

Published by Karim Hajee and Creating Power

For further information contact Creating Power at:
416-227-9665
263 Park Home Ave
Toronto, Ontario
Canada
M2R-1A1
www.creatingpower.com

Acknowledgements:

There are simply too many people to thank for making this book a reality. My gratitude goes out to every student who ever emailed me or called – their feedback and questions have allowed me to improve my ability to help others all around the world. To my father, who is no longer with us, his inspiration and passion lives on each day that I am alive. To my brother Bashir, for his endless support and encouragement. To my wife Salima, for her constant belief in me and her supportive words that help me continue each day. And of course none of this would be possible without my mother – who has taught me everything that I share with you in this book, who has been my pillar of strength and whose constant encouragement, passionate words of support and unending commitment to help others has allowed me to put together this book and all of my other material. To all of you I thank you from the bottom of my heart. To you the reader – enjoy - you're about to discover something wonderful.

Sincerely,

Karim Hajee

Power Of Believing

Table Of Contents

Power Of Believing

Introduction

> "Nothing can stop the man with the right mental attitude from achieving his goal: Nothing on earth can help the man with the wrong mental attitude."
> - Thomas Jefferson

A young man has aspirations of going to Graduate school to complete a Master's degree at New York University. He gets accepted but learns that his parents can only afford to pay for one semester — which they agree to put on their visa card. After the first semester the young man returns home from school, hoping to land a summer job to pay for the next semester's tuition — and even that may not be enough. The young man insists that he will come up with the money, fully believes that he will find a way to pay for his school tuition. After some job rejections, the young man ends up getting a terrific job, a scholarship, and a paycheck from NYU to attend and teach classes for the rest of his time at the University. The young man goes on to complete his degree, ends up getting a terrific job coming out of college and quickly builds his career, along the way he covers and breaks some of the biggest stories, winning awards and traveling the world.

That young man was me. Everything that I applied to accomplish what I just outlined and to create the life that I want, including building three successful businesses, finding the right home and meeting the right woman, I now share with you in this book. You'll also hear stories from some of my students who worked with my Creating Power system to get results and create the changes that they wanted and it's all because we developed and implemented the Power Of Believing. This book will show you how to do the same so that you begin working with the Power of Believing to create the life that you want.

By now many of you have heard that if you truly believe something will happen it will – all you have to do is believe – and success is imminent. That statement is true and it has been scientifically proven – which also means that if your beliefs are in alignment with what you want – then success is only a matter of time. While it is true that what you believe is what you get – not many people truly know how to implement the Power Of Believing in their daily lives. If you could do that you enjoy enjoy success and happiness on a regular basis.

So just how do you utilize the Power Of Believing?

How do you believe when everything around you seems to be falling apart? How do you believe when you have tried so hard for so long to achieve something but you still haven't tasted success or made any progress? How do you believe when your own experiences tell you that nothing will change? Don't dismay – there is a way to make the Power Of Believing work for you no matter what your circumstances, and in this book I will reveal a process – a simple science, simple techniques that when applied properly and correctly you will begin to utilize the Power Of Believing so that you constantly enjoy success and happiness.

I'm not asking you to adopt any religious beliefs. I'm not going to ask you to adopt a new religion or a new doctrine. I'm not going to ask you to chant a certain way at a certain time or do anything that would be deemed cult-like. I am asking you to read on and discover how to apply some simple, everyday techniques that I have taught to tens of thousands of people who have worked with my Creating Power system – techniques that will change your life – once you apply them.

The reason why you're not able to believe or why you can't believe or why you're not getting results even when you do believe is because you are not following the right formula and the right process. Believing isn't something that you simply do in your head. It is not something that you simply say.

Believing is a process that you feel and experience and if you don't work with this process when you try to improve the quality of your life – you won't get the results you're looking for.

The truth is – there exists a simple and effective method to generate the process of believing and when you incorporate the Power of Believing into your everyday life you will be able to accomplish what ever you want whenever you want.

I know this may sound too good to be true – but it's not. You see I've been teaching people how to tap into their amazing powers for over 20-years. I work with students all over the world, from all kinds of backgrounds; all of them are applying the techniques I outline in my Creating Power system. One of the most important ingredients for their success is the ability to develop a new belief system – one that allows them to believe that they can achieve their goals. Without incorporating the Power Of Believing they would stand little chance for success.

Over the past 20-years I have seen some amazing results. People who thought they couldn't achieve their goals went on to accomplish more than they dreamed and they did this by developing a new pattern of believing. In this book I'll outline the 8 Power techniques that make up the Power Of Believing so that you get on the road to enjoying success and happiness. You'll also hear questions from students and subscribers to my e-mail newsletter on topics related to the power points that I outline and you'll hear from people who increased confidence, created wealth, achieved success, found true love, you name it – they've done it – and all they did was follow the simple steps I taught them in my Creating Power system – and the key techniques are outlined in this book.

So how does this Power of Believing work and how can you utilize it to create the life you want?

It's really quite simple. You have the ability to create the life you want if you simply create a belief system that corresponds to what you want to achieve – once you do this you'll be on your way to living a successful, happy and fulfilling life.

The Power of Believing is always at work; you are always creating what you believe, because what you truly believe shapes your life. This Power of Believing is connected to your subconscious mind, which is always working for you and you are always being guided or directed in life according to what you ask – and what you ask is based on what you believe – I'll explain these concepts in greater detail throughout this book. If you don't like where you're going – then change your direction by changing the instructions you give to your subconscious mind – the instructions are your thoughts and beliefs. If you feed your subconscious negative thoughts and negative beliefs then that's what you will create. If you feed your subconscious mind thoughts and beliefs of lack, gloom, despair and worry – then that's what you will create. If you don't like where you are – decide where you want to go and create a belief system that corresponds with what you want – and your subconscious mind will help you create what you want.

Quantum physics has proven that everything that exists in the universe is made up of energy – and how we see things is based on our perception, which is ultimately based on our thoughts. Just like a chair is made up of energy, tiny molecules vibrating at a certain frequency, molecules that are not visible to the naked eye, our bodies and our thoughts are also made up of molecules vibrating at certain energy levels that are not visible to the naked eye. This understanding will become important as we continue through this book – because I'll be explaining how the Power of Believing is really about energy that attracts what you believe.

But before I go on I want to explain how this book came together, why you should continue reading it and why what I outline in this book will bring results and can lead to massive changes or improvements in your life.
You're probably wondering who I am and why you

should believe what I say. For over 20-years now I have been teaching my Creating Power system in various forms. At first I would work directly with people one-to-one. Later as my client base grew I worked with people over the phone. Finally after overwhelming requests I recorded the Creating Power system, which is now available on cds and cassettes, includes a journal and an optional course transcript. I also write a weekly newsletter that is sent out electronically to more than a hundred thousand subscribers. Each week I receive countless questions from my students and subscribers, all of them want to live a better, more fulfilling life and I answer every question. This takes up a lot of time because I even talk to my students over the phone – yes they can contact me when they have questions. When I started doing this some people thought I was crazy – offering so much of my time to people I hardly know. But I do know them – they are people who know they have more to offer and are willing to do what they can to achieve their goals and live a better life. If you're willing to do that – I'm willing to listen and help.

When I started offering my students the chance to contact me I simply wanted to give them a little more guidance so that they could get better results while working with my material. But an amazing thing happened along the way – I learned what they wanted and what they were hoping to accomplish. I discovered how many people share similar hopes, desires and dreams yet these same similar people see life in such different ways. I found out why people lack confidence, why they are crippled by fear, why they worry and how they prevent themselves from achieving their goals in so many ways – often they're not even aware of how they are destroying their own lives and the lives of those around them. But here's the best part – I also found ways for them to stop destroying their lives, how to overcome their fear and obstacles so that they live the life they want.

Throughout this book I'll be discussing how the Power of Believing can work for you or against you – regardless of your religious beliefs, background and upbringing. The Power of Believing has nothing to do with a particular religion and I won't discuss my own personal religious views or try to convince you to accept any particular religious ideas or doctrines. I will show you how to tap your own inner powers by working with some simple and effective steps. In the next few chapters you'll learn how to utilize the Power of Believing so that you constantly enjoy success and happiness.

Much of this process will rely on directing your subconscious mind by working with the Power of Believing. Amazingly most people have their subconscious mind working against them and don't even know it – thus destroying their lives. You'll learn how to re-direct your subconscious mind so that it creates the life you want. I'll also discuss the power of change and how it really is a signal for better things to come, the power of your thoughts, the power of planning, the Power Of Believing, the power of open-mindedness and how it can rapidly propel you to success, the power of now; how you can release the past and enjoy the greatest gift of all – the present moment. You'll also discover the power of patience – why you need it and how it always works for you, and lastly I'll show you how to stay motivated so that you continuously enjoy success and happiness.

Each of these power points will contribute to your success and happiness. If you leave one of them out or if you choose not to work with one of them you diminish your chances for success. Because when combined – these power points create a tremendous amount of positive energy, which goes to your success and they also help instill the Power of Believing – so that you continually enjoy success and happiness.

At the end of each chapter I've included some questions on the particular topic discussed from students and subscribers. The questions selected are those that I feel are either the most common or most relevant to the topic.

Each chapter also contains specific techniques that

will help you develop and work with the Power of Believing so that you achieve greater balance, fulfillment and live the life you want and deserve. All these techniques are practical and simple.

This book is not a cure all – there is no cure all to the challenges that life presents. Some like to look at these challenges as problems – bottom line – there is no cure all. Why not? Because life is a process and this book will help you along in the process – just like my newsletters or my Creating Power system will help you along in the process. During the process of life there will be different challenges at different times – and you will have to learn how to apply similar and different techniques to overcome these challenges. If only one technique helps you improve your life then you are better off than when you started and I would have accomplished my goal. But I know you will achieve a lot more than you expect as long as you continue working with the techniques I have outlined you will enjoy the life you want.

You may have heard of some of the concepts that I will discuss in this book – but if you read and do nothing you only have information. If you take that information and act on it you give yourself power. And if you work with the techniques that I outline in this book and follow the action exercises that I provide you will tap into your inner power and begin living the life you want. In this book I am giving you information and a method so that you know how to use that information – now it's up to you to use the power of action and follow up by practicing the techniques that I outline.

With that said I ask that you keep an open mind, read this book over and over again, apply the techniques, do the things I suggest and track your results. If you have an open mind please read on and enjoy – you're in for a real treat.

By now you're probably wondering who I am and why I claim to be an authority that will help you improve your life. First let me tell you that I am not a self-improvement guru who turned his life around by working with a few techniques. I never lived out of my car, was never overweight and out of shape (okay maybe a little overweight and a little out of shape at one point in my life), I didn't bounce from job to job searching for a way to make money and then suddenly realized that I could do that by helping people with techniques I knew nothing about, I was never unemployed for a long period of time, basically I don't have a hard-luck story to tell. I was not born with a silver spoon in my mouth, did not come from a wealthy family and did not have anybody hand me money to fund my business or my education.

I will tell you that I did overcome obstacles, I did face challenges that at times seemed daunting, I did develop and master a successful career in journalism, I have built 3 successful businesses and consulted for hundreds of others, and I will tell you that I did use all of my techniques that I am about to share with you in this book – all of which helped me create the life I have today.

In short over 30-years ago I was a kid from Kenya (in East Africa) living in Toronto, forced to make new friends in a culture that wasn't too accepting of East Indians at the time. My parents had very little (we didn't buy furniture for 3 years) but always found a way to put food on the table for my brother and me. During that 30-year period I went on to complete a Master's degree in Journalism at NYU (thanks to a scholarship and some timely coincidences – which only came about because I used my very own techniques) then went on to be an award-winning Reporter in New York. During my career I worked for ABC, CBS, NBC, CBC, and Global Television. I traveled the world and broke some of the biggest stories in the country. While being a Reporter, I also launched 3 successful businesses, which are still running today, got married to a wonderful woman, and now have a home in New York and Toronto – my 2 favorite cities. Everything I teach in my Creating Power system I used to accomplish my goals and live the life I want. While this book will not go into as much detail as my Creating Power system, it will give you some practical techniques and applications to get you started. Since I started teaching my Creating Power system I have seen thousands of people change or improve their lives by working with some very simple techniques everyday. The one thing that every student of mine, and everybody I meet has in common is that on some level they all want to change or improve their lives. This book will help get you started.

Every chapter contains a technique or a tool that you can use to create the life you want. You can choose to use one tool or use all the tools. If you work with all of the tools you'll achieve the changes and success you want a lot sooner. If you use just one tool it will take you much longer. This is how I explain it to students who work with my Creating Power system: Imagine you're in a huge rowboat and you have 20 or 30 people ready to row for you but you would have to command them and explain to them exactly what you want them to do. If you utilized all 20 or 30 rowers you would likely get to where you want to go a lot sooner. If you had just one working for you – then it would obviously take you much longer to reach your destination. Knowing that – would you choose to work with just one rower or would you work with all 20 or 30? Hopefully you made the obvious choice.

So as you go through this book make notes and work with all of the techniques. Now – let's get started.

creatingpower.com

1

Power of Thoughts And Beliefs

"The greatest revolution of our generation is the discovery that human beings, by changing the inner attitudes of their minds, can change the outer aspects of their lives."

- William James

For centuries people from all walks of life, from all parts of the world have been told that if you simply believe in yourself you can do anything. Science has also proven this to be true so now you know how to create miracles in your life – all you have to do is believe – Great! But how do you really believe when you look around and you think your life is crumbling, perhaps you're in debt and the bills are mounting, there's no food on the table, you haven't worked in months, your girlfriend /wife /boyfriend/ husband walked out on you and left you with six hungry kids? How do you believe that things are better when life seems to be a daily struggle, a grind in which from your current viewpoint you see no end in sight? How can you believe when all your experiences seem to tell you that there is no hope?

I get asked this question all of the time and my short answer is really simple: you have to believe with all your heart that things are better – or your life will never improve. That's the short answer and notice I said that you have to believe that your life *IS* better – not that it *will be better* – but that it already *IS* better. Believing that your life *IS* better is a key ingredient for your success and while I just gave you the short answer to the questions in the previous paragraph – the longer answer starts like this: believing requires that you have a feeling that life is better and you develop this feeling and belief through a process. To reach that point where you completely believe that life is better and that you can achieve your goals you build on the process each day as you strive to turn your life around until one day you have that feeling where you believe with all your heart that things are getting better and that they will continue to get better.

The process of believing isn't something that you can simply instill in yourself – you can't just wake up one day and say: "From now on – I'm going to believe that life is getting better." And expect that to last. You can't just say: "Oh, I believe – I know one day things will get better – I have hope and I believe." That's just not good enough because there's no feeling and there's no conviction, which makes the above statement wishful thinking. In order for the Power of Believing to work you have to believe with feeling, emotion and beyond a shadow of a doubt that life is better, that you can accomplish your goals and that you will continue to live the life you want no matter what is thrown at you. If there is a hint of doubt, if you don't believe for a moment – the power of believing will not work for you. And to make things worse, if you begin to believe that life will never get better – it will only get worse. You see the Power Of Believing can work for you or against you – it's up to you to decide how you want to use it.

So how do we work with the Power of Believing and how do we work with the process that allows us to utilize the Power Of Believing whenever we want?

The process of believing begins with how you see things, what you focus on and how you reward yourself as you make progress. It involves creating a belief system that is in line with what you want to accomplish.

So why is it that when you believe you can do something – you will achieve your goal?

When you believe – beyond a shadow of a doubt – you are actually sending an incredibly powerful message to your subconscious mind. You are essentially instructing it to create that which you believe. There are no instructions more powerful than your beliefs – and your subconscious will instantly act on your beliefs – because your beliefs are packed with emotion and are imbedded in your mind and psyche. This is what the subconscious picks up on and this is what it takes as an instruction. Your subconscious will follow these instructions as long as you hold those beliefs and your subconscious will shape your life based on those beliefs.

So if you believe that it is difficult to find a job – then your subconscious will create situations that make it difficult for you to find a job. If you believe that it is difficult or impossible to find the right partner – then your subconscious will make it difficult or impossible for you to find the right partner. If you believe that you are destined to fail – then your subconscious will lead you to situations where you will always fail.

Your current life is the sum total of all your beliefs. I know you may not want to accept that but it is the truth – you and you alone created the current life that you have and it is all based on your belief structure. I know some of you may say: "Karim, I haven't been able to find a job for months – yeah I believe it's difficult to find a job – wouldn't you if you were unemployed for nearly a year?" Sure you now believe that it's difficult to get a job – but did you believe it was going to be difficult when you started looking? Did you dread losing your old job and being forced to go back out and find new work – or did you look forward to the process with a tremendous amount of zest and zeal, ready to embrace a new opportunity and discover what life has to offer in the new phase that you were about to embark on? Were you open to new possibilities or were you stubborn about the kind of work you wanted – not willing to bend and try something new or different?

Your attitude and beliefs prior to the process of job hunting are what shaped your reality and before determining that the Power of Believing doesn't work you should examine your thought process and beliefs – be honest with yourself only you can change your current situation and there are no right answers – only honest answers will help you get on track.

I had a 67-year old woman call me up and ask me about my Creating Power system. She said she used to play the slot machines and when she played she always believed she was going to win and sure enough she would win. But over the years she had stopped playing and when she recently went to play the slot machines she was no longer so sure she would win – she didn't know if she could still win. Sure enough, she lost. So she wanted to know if my course would help her not only at the slot machine – but to help her in other areas of her life. She was skeptical at first but after doing the course for 4 weeks she felt much better and went to the slot machines, this time believing she would win. The first time out she won 6-thousand dollars. The second time out she won 35-hundred dollars and the third time she won 43-

hundred dollars. She only called to tell me of how things had changed since she started working with the Creating Power system after her third time at the slot machines. Now I'm not suggesting that you use the Power of Believing to win at the Casino – and I certainly don't recommend it. But you can use the Power of Believing to turn your life around.

A 35-year old man living in Tacoma, Washington emailed me explaining he had not had a job in 2 years and felt that no matter what he did he would never find work. Quite a gloomy outlook for a 35-year old and after exchanging several emails we finally had a conversation. During our conversation I learned that he didn't think he would get work because he was in the IT field and there were simply no jobs, yet he kept looking for jobs in the IT field. I was completely baffled. If you believed that there are no jobs in a certain field why would you go looking there? I asked him. He said that's all he knew, that's what he was trained to do – to work in IT so he had to find a job in IT. I suppose it makes sense on the surface but after discussing things a little further I asked him if he would consider doing something completely different. I explained that if he looked at things a little differently he would see that he wasn't compelled to find a job in the IT field. In fact he was actually at a wonderful crossroad in life – he now had the opportunity to do anything that he wanted to do – anything. When he began to look at things a little differently he realized that he really didn't want to be in the IT field anymore and he actually had a passion for Real Estate – something his father had been doing for some time. He believed that with his father's help – he could be very successful selling Commercial Real Estate. He talked to his father and within 6 months they formed a new company together – where they would share the profits of their deals. The man who once felt compelled to work in the IT field is now making a comfortable living dealing in commercial real estate.

In the above example the person believed that they could not find a job in a certain field and therefore didn't find anything for 2 years. However, he believed that he could do well if he partnered with his father and pursue a career selling Commercial Real Estate. Had he not been opened to new possibilities he would not have revealed the belief that he could do well working with his father. In this simple example you're able to see how the Power of Believing can work against you and for you – the choice is really yours.

Now I know some of you may say: "Great Karim, but I don't have a father that I can partner with to sell Real Estate. What am I supposed to do?" Start by thinking – and realizing that you have the ability to do anything you want – so what do you want to do? Think about it and we'll come back to this point in the next chapter. Right now I want to get you started in the process of applying the Power Of Believing.

The first thing you have to do is to accept that your beliefs shape your life. What you believe is what you get – it's really that simple. This of course means that you have to accept responsibility for your current life and it means that you can't blame anybody else for the way your life is. I know you may say: "my boss fired me, my wife/husband left me, my parents always put me down, I have a sick mother to care for, etc." I'm sure you can blame somebody else or some other event for the way your life is right now – but the truth is that you attracted those people and events into your life and that only happened based on your beliefs.

Sometimes a belief is not so apparent. Sometimes it can be hidden somewhere and buried in your subconscious to the point that you're not even aware of it. When you accept that your beliefs, whether you are aware of them or not, are the reason why your life is not the way you want it to be – you can then move on to the next step in the process, which is to uncover all of your beliefs and here's how you're going to do it. First grab a pen and a notepad or you can use the space provided in this book if you like. On the first page I want you to list what you would like to change in your life – put one goal or point per page. For example: If you wanted to get a new job, meet someone, buy a new home and travel – then you would put "Get a new Job" at the top of one page, on the next page you would write the next goal, which in this case would be "Meet Someone." Do this for every goal/objective that you have.

Goal One:

_____

_____

_____

_____

_____

_____

_____

_____

_____

_____

_____

_____

_____

_____

_____

_____

_____

_____

_____

Goal 2:

_____

_____

_____

_____

_____

_____

_____

_____

_____

_____

_____

_____

_____

_____

_____

_____

_____

_____

_____

Goal 3:

_____

_____

_____

_____

_____

_____

_____

_____

_____

_____

_____

_____

_____

_____

_____

_____

_____

Goal 4:

_____

_____

_____

_____

_____

_____

_____

_____

_____

_____

_____

_____

_____

_____

_____

_____

_____

I've only created 4 goals for you – but if you have more than 4 goals or more than 4 things that you want to change in your life by all means add a few more pages – create a list as long as you like – just make sure that you write out your beliefs for each of these areas that you want to improve or each of the goals that you want to accomplish. How do you find these beliefs? It's pretty simple. As you list your goals ask yourself if you think you can achieve them? How do you feel when you think about achieving those goals or creating the changes that you want in your life? For example: do you think you're not ready, not sure if you really want them, may not be able to get things done, don't have the time, don't know what to do or how to go about achieving them. These are all samples of beliefs – you shouldn't have to think too deeply – just let the responses come naturally and easily. For example: in the earlier case we had a man trained in IT but didn't believe there were any jobs in the field. He wanted to get a new job but he had a belief that there were no good jobs. Now simply list your beliefs about the goals that you want to achieve beside the goals that you've listed.

When you're done – take a look at the beliefs that you have listed and I want you to now circle all of the beliefs that do not work for you – these are the beliefs that can create the situation that you don't want. If you were honest – you would find a number of beliefs that don't work for you. For example: if you listed that you wanted to meet someone and had a belief that said "there are no good men/women in my area" then that's a limiting belief that works against you. Once you've circled these beliefs you now know what needs to change – it's the beliefs that you just circled.

Now you've just completed the first step in the process of utilizing the Power of Believing – you know what beliefs work for you and you know what beliefs don't work for you. During the rest of this book we will be changing these beliefs so that you create a new belief system that works for you and helps you create the life you want.

I promised I would share some emails from real people who are either interested in my Creating Power system or who are currently working with my Creating Power system. I get hundreds of emails everyday – I've simply selected what I feel are the most relevant and provoking emails to help you in the process.

Question:
"Karim, I've been reading your newsletters every week and I must say I enjoy them a great deal. My problem is that I always believe that something will go wrong. I set out to accomplish these great goals, I even get started, but along the way I have this strange feeling that something will go wrong and I will fail. Is this simply negative thinking?

What can I do to overcome this feeling and belief?
Please help?
-David T.

Answer:

David, what you are experiencing is negative thinking. But there is more going on. Somewhere along your journey in life something may have gone wrong when you set out to accomplish a goal. Instead of adjusting and trying a different option you may have given up and accepted that something will always go wrong. Now this line of negative thinking has led to a belief that something will always go wrong. Your subconscious mind has picked up on this belief and will attract or direct you to situations where something will go wrong. Your mind is used to this process and your subconscious mind thinks that you want something to go wrong so things always go wrong – or you stop before you even get started because you have accepted that something will go wrong. In a way something has already gone wrong because you've given up before you got started. So to change this you need to re-train the mind and re-direct the subconscious mind. The way to do this is to focus on what you want to happen, tell yourself that you are finding ways to accomplish your goals and that things are working out. Focus on making things go right, and always be open to new opportunities. Sure things won't always go smoothly – but that doesn't mean that something has gone wrong.

Instead, when things don't work out the way you planned – look at it as an opportunity to find another way to accomplish your goal – this is the process of being open to new possibilities. As you embark on your new goal encourage yourself when things go well and make changes when things don't work out the way you planned. Don't give up – focus on what you want, change the beliefs and keep moving in the direction of accomplishing your goals.

Question:
"Hi Karim,
I'm currently working with your Creating Power system and I've discovered that I have a number of negative or limiting beliefs. This scares me. Will I really be able to change these beliefs? How long will it take? Thanks for all your help."
-Cynthia S.

Answer:
Cynthia, it's okay to have negative or limiting beliefs – we all will have some limiting or negative beliefs. Now that you are aware of them – you can begin working on changing them – and then you'll begin to create the life that you really want. Instead of being scared, think of this as an opportunity to rid yourself of the negative beliefs and begin creating new beliefs – the kind that will help you accomplish your goals. How long will it take? That really is up to you. The more you work

with the techniques I've outlined, the more often you focus on changing your negative beliefs and creating positive statements, and positive beliefs the sooner you'll eliminate the negative beliefs and begin creating a new positive belief structure.

Question:
"Is there a simple process of creating new beliefs – so that I can begin achieving my goals sooner."
-Unknown

Answer:
There is no shortcut. You have to work with the process. You have to give your mind new information and give your subconscious new instructions. Think of it as re-programming your mind and subconscious, once you've done this results will quickly follow.

Question:
"Karim, ever since I was a kid my parents always put me down. My father would tell me I was good for nothing and that I would do nothing with my life. My mother rarely encouraged me. I've worked hard to prove them wrong. I teach at a University, I earn a good living, but I still hear my father's voice everyday and I sometimes believe that I will never amount to anything. How can I change this? Please help."
-Sanjay.

Answer:

Sanjay,

Your father said what he did a long time ago. You are not that person now – you are the person you have chosen to be. Instead of looking at what your father said – focus on the kind of person you are today. Take a look at your achievements and acknowledge your success. You can choose to be the person you want or you can choose to be the person your father thought you would be – it's up to you. Every time you hear your father's voice – tell yourself that you're not that person and begin looking at your accomplishments. Pat yourself on the back for what you have achieved – and do this every time you hear your father's voice. In time – that voice will fade away and you will encourage yourself to continue moving forward because you will be aware of your success and you'll know that you can build on that success each and everyday.

Question:

"Karim, I've been going through your Creating Power course and I enjoy it a great deal. I have been having some trouble coming up with goals – I just don't know what I want. I guess I'm so used to having a crappy life that I no longer know what I want. Any suggestions?"
-Amy R.

Answer:

Hi Amy,

Sometimes we get so used to things the way they are that we forget where we want to go. This seems to have happened in your situation. I suggest you start thinking about what kind of life you want. Fast forward to 5 years from now – what would your ideal life look like? Where would you be living? Who would you be with? What would you be doing? Once you start doing this you'll get a better idea of what you want. Then start breaking it down into smaller goals that you can manage and build on. For example: if you live in an apartment now and in 5 years your ideal life has you living in a house that you own – then one of your goals is to have your own home. If 5 years from now you are in a loving relationship – then another goal is to be in a loving relationship. Get the idea? You probably won't come up with all of the answers right away – but as you start thinking about what kind of life you want you'll start to get some answers. I suggest you do this regularly – everyday whenever you can – at least for a couple of weeks. By simply thinking about it you get your mind and subconscious mind moving in a different direction. Finally, instead of telling yourself that you don't know what you want – tell yourself that you do know what you want. While you may not consciously know – simply saying that you do know what you want will instruct your subconscious mind to help you come up with some answers.

2

The Power Of Planning and Goal Setting

"There are no secrets to success. It is the result of preparation, hard work, and learning from failure."
- Colin Powell

Every year I make it a point to catch up with some old friends that I don't always get to see as often as I would like. Coordinating these events is always a challenge because while everybody wants to have these little get-togethers no one ever wants to do any of the planning. Eventually a friend an I arrange the evening and during the process I'm always struck by how many people simply don't plan their lives. They'll plan everything else – but they won't plan their lives and how they want it to unfold. I find this startling – and if you're among those that haven't taken the time to plan their life – I hope that after you read this chapter you'll understand the power of planning and goal setting – and why it could tremendously increase your chances of success and achieving your goals.

Planning and setting goals is important because when you have a plan and when you have goals you give your mind and subconscious mind a set of instructions – a roadmap that you would like to follow. Your subconscious then begins following that roadmap as long as you keep it in mind and make it a priority. Simply having a plan that you never execute is pointless. Simply having goals that you have no intention of achieving is just as pointless. For your subconscious mind to act on your plan and goals you need to execute that plan and you need to continue pursuing your goals. Then only can your subconscious mind give you the guidance that you need and direct you to the opportunities that will help you fulfill your plan and achieve your goals.

How do you know you're among those that simply didn't plan their lives? Take a look at where you are now – did you plan any of it? If you did how much did you plan? What did you plan? What worked out and what part of your plan didn't work out.

I want you to take a moment now and list your answers. For example: If you planned 10-percent of your life – write that down. If you planned 20-percent of your life; write that down. If you planned your career list that – but also list what you didn't plan and how much you didn't plan. You can use the space provided in this book if you like.

How Much Of My Life I Planned:

_____
_____
_____
_____
_____
_____
_____
_____

How Much I Did Not Plan:

_____
_____
_____
_____
_____
_____
_____
_____

What I Planned That Worked Out:

_____
_____
_____
_____
_____
_____
_____

What I Planned That Did Not Work Out:

_____
_____
_____
_____
_____
_____
_____
_____

What I didn't Plan that I like:

_____
_____
_____
_____
_____
_____
_____

What I Didn't Plan That I Don't Like:

_____
_____
_____
_____
_____
_____
_____
_____

You can come back and add to this list if you like but for now I want you to take a look at how much of your life you planned and how much of your life you didn't plan. If you find that a majority of your life has been unplanned then you may also find that most of the things that you don't like are things that you didn't plan. Perhaps there will be a few situations that you did not plan that you like – but usually you'll find that most of the things that you don't like are events that you did not plan.

There will also be some things that you did plan that either didn't work out or that you don't like. This exercise is needed so that you can simply take a look on paper at how your life has progressed. There's a good chance that most of what you like was planned, at least it was planned on some level. Of course if you haven't listed anything that you like you probably need to take a closer look. If you find that there's a lot of what you don't like don't feel so bad – because the good news is that you can now change everything – after all – that's why you're reading this book.

You now know that change is going to happen – whether you want it or not. You also know that your thoughts ultimately shape your life and that your mind – filled with its thoughts and beliefs – directs your subconscious mind to create the life you want. Now you're going to learn how to create the changes you want by utilizing the power of planning and goal setting – so that your mind starts giving your subconscious mind the proper instructions – the instructions that will help you achieve your goals.

The Importance Of Planning and Goal Setting

Planning and goal setting are crucial to success in any endeavor. Sports teams have a plan and an objective or a goal before they go into any game. Military strategists have a plan and a goal before going into war. Politicians can win or lose based on their plan and how they outline their goals – if the people like their plans and goals – they will likely vote for them. People make plans to meet friends, plan their weddings, engagements, parties, social events – you even plan your trips before you go on vacation. Many of you have a plan of how you'll get to work everyday. You have a goal in the morning, which is to get to work and you follow a plan or routine that will get you there. Chances are that if you look back you'll find that events that went smoothly and were a lot of fun – were likely well planned and there was a particular goal in mind. You likely get to work on time everyday because you follow a certain plan – one that will allow you to reach the goal of getting to work on time – your plan is typically your routine. During this routine you know what time to get up, have breakfast, and what route to take to get to work on time (your goal). Along the way – as with any plan – you may make some adjustments – but your goal is clear – to get to work at a specific time.

So if you have success with some of the little and some of the big goals that you plan – why not use that same approach in life? If it is effective on a small scale – it will likely be just as effective on a larger scale. I'm always amazed when I hear people tell me "I don't have a goal or a plan – I guess I'll figure it out when I get there." Huh? How can you get somewhere when you don't know where you're going? What will you figure out and when? Would you say that about your wedding? Think about it. Would you tell everybody to show up at a hall for your wedding reception and not have a hall in mind and have no plan for what to do? No. Would you drive off to work without a plan as to what road to take or how you will get there? No. Would you get in your car and just start driving with no particular destination (goal) in mind? No. So why would you go through life without any goals and no plan? After all – it's your life and you don't have any idea what you want to achieve with it and you have no plan for what you're going to do with this wonderful opportunity you have. No wonder nothing works out!! How can anything work out when you don't know what you want to work out or how you can make it work out?

If you want to succeed at anything – you have to have an objective – a goal and you have to have a plan. If you want to have a successful business – you need to know what the goal of that business is, what would define success for that business and a business plan that you could follow and execute. If you want to have a successful life then define your goals and get a plan together – otherwise you're going to be busy reacting to situations your whole life and you'll never achieve your success because you simply didn't take the time to decide what that success is and you didn't have a plan to follow.

Students who work with my Creating Power system learn to get a plan together in the very first week. This is crucial to their success – some plan as far ahead as 10 or 20 years. Now I know not all of you want to plan 10 or 20 years in advance but if you could come up with a 5 year plan – one that is filled with goals that allow you to enjoy success and happiness you'll begin to improve your life tremendously.

Why Goal Setting And Planning Leads to Success

When you set a goal and make a plan – you have a clear vision – you know exactly what you want to accomplish, what you need to do and how everything can start to come together. If you were to plan a wedding you would go through all the fine details – right down to the very last thing that may seem to be the least important to most people. When you prepare for a game you go in with a plan – your team knows what it has to do and has a plan that the coaching staff is confident will lead to victory. Teams that go in without a plan – rarely, if ever, win. I'll give you a personal example of how planning can lead to dramatic improvements. While I was growing up I played soccer regularly and competitively. We had a good group of friends and we created our own team. In our very first year we didn't have a coach and we won our championship. We thought we didn't need a coach – we could coach ourselves – who needs a plan? We could just go out and play and win. Well, that didn't work – ever again. We would get to the finals and lose. We would get to the semi-finals and lose. Finally we got a coach who came up with a plan, instilled discipline and forced us to follow and stick with the plan. We started winning championships again. This same process applies in life – without a plan, without discipline, without sticking to the plan you stand little or no chance of succeeding. Losing in the finals is not good enough – no one remembers the team that came in second.

When you set a goal and make a plan you plant this vision in your mind and you also plant it in your subconscious mind. Your subconscious mind now says: "Aha – we have a goal and we have a plan – let's follow it." As long as you keep your mind focused on the goal and the plan you will succeed. The plan may change from time to time – and if you adjust course and go with what works your chances for success will increase dramatically as long as you have the goal in mind – because by staying focused on your goal you constantly send information to your subconscious – you're constantly telling your subconscious mind that this is important and we better keep working on it. Your subconscious then creates the opportunities for you to achieve that goal.

To succeed in life – set your goals, get a plan and stay focused – if you lose focus you lose sight of the goal, you then forget about the plan and before you know it everything falls apart. Why? Because you have stopped focusing on the goal and in so doing you stopped telling your subconscious that the goal is important. By not focusing on your goal you stopped telling your subconscious to continue working on making your particular goal a reality.

Imagine planning a party for 200 people. Think of all the details that have to be considered and as you plan this event there is a good chance that you would be focused on that event and the details everyday – you would be making sure everything was taken care of. Your focus on your goal of having the event and your plan is what your subconscious picks up and forces you to check everything over and over again until you've got it right. If it's not right you'll make the proper changes. If you're the kind of person who simply can't plan a luncheon for 3 people then you have some work to do – and the good news is you can begin to work with the power of planning and goal setting so that you turn things around and improve your life dramatically.

Now start using the same approach in life. Come up with your goals, devise a plan and stay focused. This is something I constantly teach my students who work with my Creating Power system – they learn to choose their goals, devise a plan and stay focused because they are constantly sending the right messages to their subconscious mind – this allows them to achieve success. It also creates opportunities for them – and they in turn – learn how to follow up on those opportunities by relying on intuition and their subconscious mind. By doing what I've just outlined you'll be taking the first concrete steps to achieving your goals and you'll also have a clear idea of what is important and how you plan to get there.

Whenever I talk about goal setting and planning I always have someone calling me or emailing me to tell me that they don't know what their goals are or they don't know how to come up with a plan. So now I'm about to outline how you can select your goals and begin creating a plan.

If you don't have any goals, if you don't want to come up with any goals, if you feel that there is no reason to set goals and prefer to just sort of free-flow through life – then you're probably not going to achieve a lot and you probably won't get a lot out of life. But if you want to enjoy life, if you want to enjoy success, if you want to have a better life then you should set some goals and come up with a plan.

The first thing I tell all of my students who work with my Creating Power system is that if they want to set goals then you should look at where you are now and what kind of life you want to have. You should try to look at what kind of life you want in 6-months, a year, 5 years, 10 years, 20 years and possibly 30 years. But you should also be realistic about your goals and I say this not to discourage you – but to help you understand that there is a process at work and that process most often doesn't create the results you want overnight. You may feel that you want things to change right away – that these changes *have to* happen right away – but you should understand and accept that you created the situation you are in, it took you a long time to get here and you'll have to give yourself some time to get out of the mess that you're in. Can things turn around right away? Sure they can. Is it realistic? No.

I often hear from people who want to be millionaires but don't have a job. Now there's nothing wrong with wanting to be a millionaire when you don't have a job – in fact it's great that they have lofty aspirations – at least they have a desire to improve their life. But in many cases these people want to be millionaires within 3 months or 6 months. Sure it's possible – after all I'm a firm believer that anything is possible. When I ask them to think of how they can achieve this goal, when I ask them to come up with a plan to make a million dollars – here's the most common answer: "I'll win the lottery." Yes this too is possible. But is it likely? What are you going up against? What can you do to make a million dollars besides buy lottery tickets? Why limit yourself to just one way of making a million dollars when there are so many other ways to make a million dollars? I firmly believe that we are all here for a reason – that we all have the ability to make as much money as we want, that we all can live wonderful happy lives and enjoy success and happiness if we work with the process of life and allow our spirit or our higher self to guide us along the way. Some people will win the lottery – but there will be many more people who will make their millions in other ways. When you focus only on winning the lottery you limit yourself to one possibility. When you focus on making a million dollars and are open to accomplishing that goal in any number of ways – you allow yourself to grow and live a life with purpose. More importantly you give your subconscious mind the option to guide you to the best way for you to make a million dollars. Don't limit yourself to just one possibility. Yes come up with a plan – but be open to all possibilities because you never know exactly how you will achieve your goals.

I'll give you a personal example. When I started my career as a journalist I had just finished my Graduate Degree at NYU and I was on my way to Vancouver, British Columbia to work at a local television station. After spending 2 years in New York I knew that I wanted to live in Manhattan and be a Reporter in New York. But getting a job as a Reporter in New York straight out of Graduate school was a long shot. Sure I tried – but I had no luck. The only concrete job offer I got – came from a station in Vancouver, British Columbia – the opposite end of the country – nowhere near where I wanted to be. My mind was focused on getting to New York and I made it a priority to get back to New York. Sure, Vancouver is a beautiful city – but it wasn't New York. One day, while working in Vancouver, I learned of a conference for journalists taking place in Seattle, Washington – a 2-hour drive from Vancouver. All the top executives from all the major stations including New York would be there. If I registered early enough I would be able to meet with them and the top recruiters for some of the biggest stations in New York. I signed up and armed with my resume and several videotape copies of my work I hopped into my car and drove down to Seattle. I had met with just about everybody and I kept getting the same response from all of them – I wasn't ready and needed some more experience. Finally I met with Steve Paulus who was the Assistant News Director at WCBS Television in New York. Steve is a big hockey fan and he identified my Canadian background with hockey. He said while he liked my work – I wasn't quite ready but he wanted me to stay in touch. Dejected and disheartened I drove back to Vancouver while contemplating my future. I decided that I would do what I had to so that I could get back to New York. If I needed more experience – I would get it, if I had to stay in Vancouver to get that experience I would stay in Vancouver for as long as it took.

A few months later my friends in New York asked me to visit and spend New Year's Eve with them. I agreed. But the day that I was supposed to return to Vancouver we had a snowstorm in New York and my flight was cancelled. Later in the day, while I was still in New York, an old friend who was also working as a Reporter just outside New York called to say hi – he had heard I was in town and wanted to get caught up. During our conversation he told me that a new all news station was starting up in New York, which was being funded by Time Warner. I asked him who was in charge of the operation and he said a man by the name of Steve Paulus was the News Director. I almost fell over. Before returning to Vancouver I called Steve who remembered me as the Canuck. He said while he didn't think I was a good fit at WCBS – he thought I would work well in his new station. Within 4 months he offered me a job and I was back in New York. This only happened because I stayed focused on my goal to get back to New York and was open to any and all possibilities. While working for Steve I broke some of the biggest stories in the country, which catapulted my career. When you are focused on your goal, when you are open to all possibilities and you follow the process – you will succeed.

For those who want to make a million dollars the answer to accomplishing that goal isn't in buying more lottery tickets. The answer to being a millionaire and making millions of dollars is inside you – you have the answer – you just have to uncover it. We all have the ability to have what we want and more but only if we allow ourselves to work at our full potential, stay focused on our goals and work with the process of life and allow your subconscious to guide you. When you do this – your mind, spirit and body are all working together to make the outcome you are seeking a reality. They are all working to help you achieve your goals. Your subconscious also gets going because it needs to keep up with the rest of you and it in turn starts creating new opportunities for you. By staying focused on your goal you say to your subconscious "hey – I'm ready to do my part." But when you say; "I'll just buy more lottery tickets." You're really saying: "I'm only willing to make money this one way, I'm too lazy to bother working and I'm not interested in any other possibilities." I said earlier that we all have a reason for being here – if your reason is something other than winning the lottery and you insist on buying lottery tickets then you've just limited your chances of making a million dollars. You've closed yourself off to any other possibility of making a million dollars. You would be wise to give yourself the chance to make a million dollars in any number of ways. Don't decide that you're too old, or not smart enough, or don't know how – focus on what you want to achieve and you'll find a way.

Don't get me wrong – I know of people who have focused on and won the lottery, but while they were buying lottery tickets they were also focusing on finding new ways to make a million dollars. They didn't limit themselves to just winning the lottery.

Here's an example of how being open to all possibilities can help you achieve more than what you want. A student working with my Creating Power system, had been working with his father on and off in his father's business. He wasn't sure if he wanted to continue when he started taking my course. During one of our email exchanges I suggested that he think about what he wanted and then focus on making that happen while working with the rest of the techniques that I outlined in my Creating Power system. He explained that he wanted to make millions and after thinking things through he decided to continue working with his father and work with the Creating Power system. By the end of the year they had doubled their revenue and the following year they were looking at building on that. He wasn't making just a few thousand dollars more – he started making millions.

This student succeeded because he made a choice, came up with a plan, focused on it and stayed committed to achieving his goal. He was also open to new possibilities and looked at a lot of opportunities before making his decision. Sure my Creating Power system helped – but it only helped him uncover his true potential.

Now I also hear from people who are making 30-thousand dollars a year who want to make a million dollars within 6-months. Yes anything is possible – but you also have to give yourself a realistic chance. In the case of the gentleman who worked with his father – they were in an industry that can be very lucrative. He also had the benefit of drawing on his father's years of experience to guide him through the process – but he had a goal and was able to recognize an opportunity and embrace the change.

Look at it this way – you're about to run a marathon – but you've never trained to run in a marathon, and you've never trained to run more than a hundred yards. Now suddenly you want to run 20+ miles – and you expect to win – but you've never trained. Is it likely? It is possible – but is it likely? Wouldn't you be better off training, getting in shape, then start by running a mile, 2 miles, 4 miles, 8 miles until you got to the point where you were running 20+ miles – before you entered the race?

If you want to be successful – you have to prepare, train and take things one step at a time while setting realistic goals that you can build on. If you want to be a millionaire and you currently don't have a job – start by getting a job or starting a business. If you currently make 30-thousand a year and you want to be a millionaire – how about increasing your yearly income first? Perhaps aim for making an additional 15-thousand a year either by getting a promotion, a raise, another better paying job, or by doing something in addition to what you are currently doing – find something that would allow you to make some extra money. Then increase that, and continue increasing it until you get to a million.

If you want to get out of debt – then start by paying off a small amount of your debt – then increase the amount you pay off. If you want to meet the right person – start by going out, then getting to know people until you meet the person you think is right for you.

When you keep your goals realistic and take things one-step at a time – 2 things happen. First you start building your confidence – which is crucial to your success. Next you start sending the message to your subconscious mind that you're ready for change and you're embracing change. You start telling your subconscious that you can do this, you say you are improving and you are ready for change and that you are giving your subconscious mind and your power within the time needed to help you achieve your goals and create the changes or improvements you want in life.

Keep Your Mind Focused

Now I've discussed setting goals, making a plan and taking things one-step at a time in order to make progress and build confidence. Another crucial element in the process of setting and planning goals is the ability to keep your mind focused on your goals. If you don't keep your mind focused on what you want to achieve – you'll never get anything done.

Think of your mind as an entity on it's own – as though it is completely separated from you. There's you who wants certain things and would like to achieve certain goals. And there's your mind – which is used to doing things it's own way and is certainly not used to you telling it what to do.

As you try to get your mind to focus on what you want it will try to convince you to give up. Your mind will put up all kinds of resistance – it will tell you that there's no need to change, that things are fine just the way they are. Your mind will tell you that you don't have time right now to do the things you need to do to create the changes that you want. It will tell you - it's no use, things will never get better. Or it will try to convince you to put things off until later – do it later. When the mind does this it's simply deceiving you – it's simply trying to get you to stop and avoid change. The mind does this because it doesn't want change. It wants things to stay the way they are – it's happy in its misery. But you're not. You want change – except your mind is not letting you change. If you don't stay focused you'll give in to your mind and the idea that you can't improve your life, in the end nothing ever gets better.

So how do you get your mind to listen and agree to the changes? First start by sticking with your commitment, think of your goals, when change arrives – look for the opportunities, embrace and welcome change – after all if you want to improve your life things are going to have to change. Do this everyday and you'll see your mind starting to adjust. Set realistic goals and as you achieve smaller goals – acknowledge your success. Finally – understand that getting your mind to change and work in a different way is a process. Just like you're not going to run 20-miles in a day your first time running – your mind is not going to adjust and change overnight. There is a process at work and students who work with my Creating Power system understand this process because they work with daily exercises to help them train their mind.

If you want your mind to work for you – then you have to push it in a new direction. If you don't you'll never see the changes you want. Why do you have to get your mind to work differently? Because your mind is a direct link to your subconscious mind – if you want to unlock the power of your subconscious – if you want to achieve your goals – then your mind has to be focused, directed and committed to those goals. Your subconscious will only create what your mind regularly thinks and what you believe.

When you resist change – you basically say that you don't want to improve your life; that you don't want opportunities that will allow you to live the life you want. Everyday you are presented with new opportunities – just one of them could drastically help you improve your life. Don't miss out on the opportunity just because you're stubborn.

Setting Goals.

Earlier I suggested that if you want to better understand what your goals are you should think of what kind of life you want in the next 6 months, year, 2 years, 5 years, 10 years, 20 years and 30 years. Now I want you to outline your goals. So think about the kind of life that you want and list your goals. For example: if you want to be making a million dollars in 5-years – make that a goal. If you want to own a new home in 2-years make that a goal. If you want to get a new job in 6-months make that a goal. If you want to get out of debt in a year – then make that a goal. Think about your goals and start listing them. Don't take this exercise lightly. Scientific studies show that people who write down their goals are 80-percent more likely to achieve them than those that do not write down their goals. By simply writing your goals you increase your chances by 80-percent. So you can use the space provided or you can use a separate journal to list your goals.

Goals:

_____

_____

_____

_____

_____

_____

_____

_____

_____

_____

_____

_____

_____

_____

_____

_____

_____

_____

_____

Great – you have some goals and this is the beginning of creating your new life. Now I want you to go back and review your goals and get more specific. For example: if you said you wanted to make more money in the next 12 months – then get more specific by saying how much more you want to make. If you want to eliminate your debt – how much of your debt do you want to eliminate. If you want to get a job then what kind of job and how much will it pay. Go back to your list and get more specific.

Now I want you to break your goals down into smaller more manageable goals and by this I mean look at what is the first step that needs to be done. For example: if you want to get married - then the first step would be to be in a relationship, improve the one you're in and spend more time with the person you hope to marry. If you want to get out of debt and payoff the bills - then the first step would be to cut back on spending, save some money and start paying off some of the bills. If you want to get back in shape - then the first step would be to lose some weight, eat better, and start working out. Get the idea?

Whatever your ultimate goal is – break it down into smaller, more manageable goals. Then as you achieve these smaller goals you build your confidence, you start to feel better about yourself and most importantly – you begin to make progress toward achieving your goal.

Students who work with my Creating Power system begin focusing on their goals and setting the smaller goals within the first week. This an important exercise that you're now going to follow. So let's break your goals down into smaller more manageable goals – and you're going to do this by outlining the first steps you need to take in order to achieve your goals.

Steps for Achieving Goals:

_____

_____

_____

_____

_____

_____

_____

_____

_____

_____

_____

_____

_____

_____

_____

_____

_____

_____

_____

_____

_____

_____

_____

_____

_____

Congratulations – you now have your goals and you have a plan. You have your roadmap – you know what you want to achieve and what steps you need to take in order to achieve those goals.

Focus On The Rewards

The next step in the goal setting and planning process is to decide why these goals are important – these are the rewards that come with achieving your goals – something I discuss in great detail in my Creating Power system.

Saying you want a million dollars just so you can buy a new home and car is not the only reason that you want to make a million dollars. Having security, comfort, peace-of-mind are more likely the reasons why you want a million dollars. Let's face it – if you had a million dollars but couldn't do anything with it the money would be useless. The reward is what you can do with the money, and how you could use the money to improve the quality of your life. If you want to be in a healthy relationship then ask yourself why – keep asking yourself why until you get the final answer – which is usually to enjoy and express love, security, to be cared for and to care – get the idea? Once you know why these goals are important to you – your motivation to achieve these goals increases dramatically. It's not the goals themselves – but what they bring or the rewards that come with achieving these goals – that's what truly motivates you.

Throughout the day – keep in mind those rewards – keep in mind the real reason those goals are important and you'll get more motivated. Too often I see people set goals and then instead of focusing on the reason – or the rewards of these goals they focus on the little things that have to get done in order to achieve them. These little things are important – but if you only focus on the tedious things that have to get done in order to achieve your goals you'll lose your motivation. For example: If you want to get back in shape and your reason for doing this is to be healthy, energetic, and to be able to enjoy the physical aspects of life – then don't focus on the fact that you have to get up and go to the gym every morning. Yes you do have to exercise – but think of the reward – think of how much your life would improve by exercising and getting back in shape – don't focus on the fact that you have to exercise. Get the idea? In the space provided I want you to list your goals and why they are important.

Goals and Why They Are Important:

_____

_____

_____

_____

_____

_____
_____
_____
_____
_____
_____
_____
_____
_____
_____
_____
_____
_____
_____
_____
_____
_____
_____
_____
_____
_____
_____
_____
_____
_____

Now that you know why these goals are important
you have your motivating factors for achieving
these goals. When you think of your goals

remember why they are important and how achieving them will change your life. By doing this you are more likely to follow through on the tedious things that need to be done in order to achieve your goals because you have the bigger picture in mind.

This process is one reason why some of the most successful people in the world have achieved their goals. They understand that there is a greater goal that needs to be achieved and that doing the smaller, tedious and annoying things is part of the process and the way they get through it is by keeping their eye on the bigger goal and why it is so important.

Achieving Your Goals

Now being motivated is great – but you have to do things to achieve those goals – and here you have to take action. Even doing little things everyday toward achieving those goals is action. Now that you have your list of goals and you know why they are important to you it's now time to come up with a plan of action. There are two forms of action you need to take – one is the physical and the other is the mental. Let's talk about the physical first.

Think about all the things you can do to make those goals a reality. If you want to make more money, meet someone, lose weight, get into shape, get a better job, spend more time with your family, stop worrying – then think about what you can do to make that happen. Write it down. Saying I don't know is not good enough. Saying I've tried everything isn't acceptable either because there's always a way and I doubt that you have truly tried everything! You just have to find the solution, the process and action that works for you. If you really think you've tried everything – write down everything you've tried and see how long that list really is. Then talk to someone who has achieved the goal that you set out to achieve and see if they did something that you haven't done yet. Chances are you'll discover something you haven't tried.

So in the space provided start listing the goals and the actions that you can take to achieve your goals.

Goals and Actions:

_____
_____
_____
_____
_____
_____
_____
_____
_____
_____
_____

_____
_____
_____
_____
_____
_____
_____
_____
_____
_____
_____
_____
_____
_____
_____
_____
_____
_____
_____
_____
_____
_____
_____
_____
_____
_____
_____
_____
_____
_____

_____

_____

_____

_____

Always think about what you can do and keep adding to that list. Then start following those steps – take the action necessary to achieve your goals. Make it a daily habit to do at least three things everyday to achieve your goals.

The next and perhaps most important step is to train your mind to send the right messages to your subconscious mind – so that you achieve your goals. You won't be able to achieve all your goals if you don't believe that you can achieve them. You could have wonderful goals and noble reasons for achieving those goals – but if you don't believe that you can achieve them – you won't.

So first examine your beliefs about your goals. Do you think you can achieve them? Do you think it would be difficult? Any negative beliefs will limit your ability to achieve your goals. If you have negative or limiting beliefs about your goals then you need to change them – you need to feed your mind the possibilities and send the right messages to your subconscious mind. What seems difficult should be considered easy. What you think you can't do should become something that you can do. What you don't believe is possible should become something you believe is possible. For example: if you want to meet someone but think it's difficult to meet people – then you need to change that statement to: it's easy to meet people. If you want to make more money but don't know how – then you need to change that to: I know how to make more money. If you want to get a promotion but think there's too much competition or that you're not qualified then you need to change the statements to: I can get a promotion and I am qualified to get a promotion. When you follow your plan of action and send the right messages to your subconscious mind you'll then begin to create opportunities for you to achieve your goals. These are new, positive affirmations that you can create and work with at anytime. Any negative belief or any negative thought pattern related to achieving your goals has to be eliminated – otherwise you don't stand a chance of achieving your goals. You could do everything else that I've outlined – but if you have a negative belief pattern related to achieving your goals – you will not succeed.

It's really that simple.

So create positive affirmations and say them as often as you can – this will help train the mind and help create new beliefs.

In the space provided outline your goals and the beliefs that you have about these goals.

Goals and Beliefs:

_____

_____

_____

_____

_____

_____

_____

_____

_____

_____

_____

_____

_____

_____

_____

_____

_____

_____

_____

_____

_____

_____

_____

_____

_____

_____

_____

_____

_____

_____

_____

Now in the following space I want you to list all of the negative or limiting beliefs that you have about your goals and change them to positive statements about achieving your goals – these become your new, positive affirmations.

Negative and Positive Beliefs for Goals:

_____

_____

_____

_____

_____

_____

_____

_____

_____

_____

_____

_____

_____

_____

_____

_____

_____

_____

_____

_____

_____

_____

_____

_____

_____

_____

_____

_____

_____

_____

_____

_____

_____

_____

_____

_____

You now have a series of statements, affirmations and thoughts that you can work with in order to help you achieve your goals. When you think about your goals and when the negative statements and beliefs enter your mind – change them to the positive statements and thoughts that you have just created. Continually work with these statements throughout the day.

Getting Results

Things won't happen overnight – although I've seen some students get terrific results in a few weeks. You may not achieve your goals in the first few days or even the first few weeks but you will see changes happening. Work within the time frame that you have set for achieving goals and remember – deadlines can be changed – and are only a guideline. If you don't achieve your goal in the time that you set don't get discouraged. Instead, measure the progress and set a new time frame for you to achieve your goals. This is part of the process – some people will get results sooner, some will take longer. Some people will finish a marathon, others will drop out. Aim to finish and you'll increase your chances of success.

Planning and Preparing

Now that you have your goals in place, now that you have a plan and now that you are training your mind for success you should begin preparing. This part of the process requires that you start living as though you've achieved your goals. I'm not saying you should go out and buy that big house or buy that new car – but mentally think as though you've achieved your goals. Do this everyday and you'll begin to see some real changes. Stay focused, get your mind and subconscious mind working for you and you'll achieve your goals in no time.

So you have goals and you have plans what I am about to say may throw you off – it may make you scratch your head and wonder why you went through the process of setting goals and planning your life. At the very beginning of this book I said that life is a process – that there is constant change and a large part of your success depends on how you approach this process. While you have goals and you have a plan you should always be open to all possibilities. Don't be married to the notion that things have to be a certain way in order for you to be happy. Don't set conditions on life – accept life and work with it. Bend when the strong winds of change blow in your path. Change your perception so that you can mould life to what you want – understand that what you desire today will change in a few years and you will adjust course. Let go of past beliefs – give yourself a fresh new start everyday. Make today a new beginning and understand that all that you want in life at this time already exists. Think about what I just said. Take a look at your attitudes – are you open minded or stubborn? Do you hang on to the past or embrace the future? Are you ready for change or is change simply going to happen with or without you?

Start embracing change, see opportunities everywhere and today grab a notepad and pen and write down three new opportunities that you discovered or three new things you learned or three new perceptions that you have adopted. The more open minded you are the longer your list will be.

Your plan can change at anytime. Perhaps you think that you're going to make a million dollars by starting a business but then a friend could come along and ask you to partner with him – it would be in your best interest to consider the opportunity and look into it further. Your goals should stay constant – don't change them too often – think about them and stick with them. But also understand that your goals today will likely change in 5 years and that is acceptable because what is a priority today may not be a priority in five years.

You have a number of exercises to work with in this chapter and the rest of this book will teach you how to train your mind for success and how to direct your subconscious mind to help you achieve those goals.

Here now are some questions from students and my newsletter subscribers on the subject of setting and planning goals.

Question:
"Karim, I understand that I need to have goals – but it seems I have too many. I sat down yesterday and came up with a list of 35 goals. Is this too much? I think so. What should I do?"
Nikos.

Answer:

Nikos, it's great that you have goals and so many aspirations. Don't be discouraged by the number. First decide what are the priorities. Take a look at your list of 35 goals and decide which are the most important and which goals you want to accomplish first. If you still find it challenging – then think about which goals would make the most dramatic improvements in your life – and focus on those first. Then take a look at the rest of your goals – chances are you'll find that many of them can be combined. If you still have a lot of goals left – then again prioritize, put them into different categories and see which are most important, which can be accomplished the soonest and which goals may take a little longer. Then decide which goals you want to complete first or right away and which goals you want to accomplish over a period of time. Remember to be realistic in your time frame and understand that deadlines can be changed. Keep an open mind and go one step at a time.

Question:

"I've been told that I need to set goals for years – but I just can't decide what I want. Am I hopeless? What can I do? Any advice would be helpful. Thanks."
Tanya S.

Answer:

Hi Tanya, deciding what you want is very important but sometimes we give the process of deciding too much importance. We get so concerned that we may choose the wrong thing that we end up making no decision. This may be something that you are experiencing. I suggest you think about your ideal life and take into consideration all the little things that you would want in this ideal life. For example; would your ideal life mean having more time to yourself, a new home, a family, the freedom to travel, financial stability – a consistent supply of income? Think about it and write down what you come up with. Follow the exercises I just outlined. When you have a list you have something to work with – you have an idea of what you want. Then you can start refining that idea, fine tune that list, get more specific, start setting smaller goals that would help you accomplish the greater goal, decide the action steps, start training your mind and directing your subconscious mind to help you achieve those goals. Another suggestion is that you stop focusing on the idea that you don't know what you want – but to instead tell yourself that you do know what you want to achieve. The truth is you do know what you want – you just haven't uncovered it. So you can work with the following affirmation: I know what I want to do with my life and I know what I want to achieve. Say that affirmation every time you think you don't know what you want to do with your life. It will help get the mind focused on discovering what you want and your subconscious mind will guide you to achieving what you want and what is best for you. This is the process of discovery – remember to keep an open mind and know that when you are open to all possibilities – then can anything happen.

Question:

"Karim, I need to change things right now. I understand your approach – but have you got any suggestions for those of us who need to change things right away. I have bill collectors knocking at my door, I don't have a job, and I could lose my home soon. How can you help me?"
Joseph.

Answer:

Hi Joseph,
First decide what it is you want and put your full effort and energy into accomplishing your top priority. Can you turn things around? Yes. Can it happen overnight? Yes but highly unlikely. You're in the situation that you're in because a number of events came about – now you need to create a number of situations that will help you turn things around. The only way to do that is to focus on what you want, direct your mind and subconscious mind to find solutions. You say you have bill collectors knocking on your door – what do you want to happen in this situation? Do you want

them to simply vanish? Do you want to pay them off all at once? Or do you want to find a solution to pay them off and keep your home? There are a number of solutions to any problem that you face – you have to first decide which solution works best for you and which outcome you want. Then begin directing your mind and subconscious mind to help you come up with the answers. A lot of what has happened has been the result of negative thinking that created the negative situation that you're in. Now it's time to change that pattern of negative thinking. Clearly it isn't working and it isn't helping you. The sooner you get started, the more disciplined you are and the more often you work with training your mind and directing your subconscious mind the sooner you'll get results.

Question:
"Karim, I'm 67 years old and feel that life has passed me by. Now you suggest I set goals – okay. I would like to have an abundance of money – but given that I'm 67 years old I may not have the luxury of time. I think buying lottery tickets is the only way. What do you suggest?"- Doris N.

Answer:
Hi Doris,
You're not 67-years old – you're actually 67-years young. You know that old saying: you're as young as you feel – but I like to think that you're always young – but wiser. You say you want abundance

but you're concerned about time and that lottery tickets may be the only way. The truth is you don't know how much time you have – but what if you thought of it as having as much time as you need. First I would suggest that you define abundance – do you need millions all at once or would you prefer a steady supply of income that would allow you to live a comfortable life? If you don't believe that you have the ability to make more money or come up with goals that you can accomplish – you won't. You want inspiration – how about Clint Eastwood who at the time of writing this was 73 and still going strong having won another Academy Award. His best work could be yet to come. Doris, it's all in how you see things. Start looking at all of the possibilities and you'll find the solutions that you're looking for. You could find a way to make a comfortable living in a relatively short period of time. Think about what you want to achieve and start setting those goals – because you could live to 95 – so how would you like the next 28-years to unfold. You may have more time than you know, you may have less – but the key is to make the most of that time, enjoy it, embrace it – do what you love and keep moving forward. Setting goals is just one step – the best part is the process of achieving them. When you look at it in a different way – time doesn't seem to have so much of an impact. I have an 84-year old student who just started a business – his third business and he has every intention of seeing it turn a profit and provide him with additional wealth. You really are 67-years young.

Question:

"I can't seem to focus on anything. I have goals – but I often forget about them and then get caught up in the daily grind. When I look back I had lots of goals – but I just can't stay focused or find a way to make them happen. What should I do?"
Terry W.

Answer:

Terry, one of the main reasons you're losing focus of your goals and not following through is not because you're getting distracted by the daily grind. More likely it's because you're not focusing on why your goals are important. I suggest you take a look at your goals and then decide why you want to achieve them – then focus on the reason and not just the goal. For example: your goal may be to start a business – but why do you want to do this? Let's say you wanted to start a business so that you didn't have to deal with the daily grind of working, or going to a job and being responsible to somebody else. Perhaps a benefit of having your own business is so that you can have the freedom to come and go as you please, be able to generate more money and be in control of your life and finances. If that's the case then focus on these benefits and when you think about improving your life and creating changes – focus on how those changes will help you, how those changes and improvements would enhance your life. Another reason you lose sight of your goals is because your mind is not used to focusing on your goals and instead is used to dealing with the daily grind. Getting it to change focus and work differently is important to your success – because when your mind is focused on your goals your subconscious mind is also focused on your goals and will begin creating the opportunities to help you achieve those goals. So focus on the rewards of your goals, train your mind to focus on your goals and begin directing your subconscious mind to create the life you want.

Question:

Karim, I have goals but I don't have time to do the things I need to do in order to achieve my goals. I work 10-12 hours a day, spend a couple of hours in the gym, when I get home I have to clean up and cook, I simply have no time left to work on achieving my goals. Any advice?
-David.

Answer:

David, this is a common problem or more likely a common excuse. First – your mind has gotten used to your daily routine and refuses to break the pattern – that's why anytime you try you fail. You have to convince your mind that change is for the better – you can do this by working with some of the techniques I've outlined. Next – and this is also part of training the mind and subconscious mind – you have to decide how important your goals are. If you're saying you have no time for them – then you're really saying that your goals are just not important enough. You need to prioritize and realize why these goals are important – remember it's the why that motivates you. If you don't know why you want to achieve them, you're likely not going to make them important enough to change your routine. Yes you have a busy schedule – but once you decide that your goals are important – you'll find the time to do the things that you have to do to achieve them.

3

The Power Of Change

After going through the first 2 chapters you now have a better idea of your beliefs, thoughts, what you want to accomplish and what thoughts you need to regularly have in order to accomplish your goals. If you work with the exercises I outlined regularly you will see changes and in this chapter I'm going to outline the Power of Change and how change can always be to your benefit – no matter what the change is – it will always be to your benefit if you work with the Power of Change. Unfortunately too many people don't utilize this power and often they resist change or do everything they can to turn away the power of change – without even realizing that they are turning away a tremendous power that can help them create the life they want.

Think of life as something that constantly evolves, you could look at it as almost claylike, because it is something that you can mould into what ever you want. But unlike clay, life never becomes permanent and it rarely stays the same. There are times when you feel like you personally haven't made the kind of progress you want but if you look carefully you will see that everything has changed. Life constantly shifts on it's own and if you want to mould it into something special you must learn how to work with the process of life in a special way and you must also learn how to cope with it's shifting nature. Life changes, and if you don't adjust course you'll lose out on some tremendous opportunities that could dramatically improve the quality of your life and the lives of those closest to you.

We all have the ability and power to create the changes we want in life – these can be short-term or long-term changes – and the process begins with a decision. But before you make the decision you first have to understand that change can happen in an instant – and change can also take time. At all times you should be prepared for change so that it doesn't come at you from left field.

Too often I hear from people who want changes in their lives and when those changes take place they decide they're not ready for it and instead of embracing the change – they put up a fight – often this is a fruitless fight because once change knocks on your door – there's virtually nothing you can do to turn it away. By putting up a fight you resist change and in the end turn away a tremendous opportunity or you fail to recognize the opportunities brought by change. In the end you fail to work with the Power of Change.

Change happens everyday, today is different from yesterday, some parts of you have changed overnight, your hair has grown, your body is a little older, you've changed your clothes, your appearance has changed in some ways – the plants and trees outside your home have changed – they've grown older, everything changes. Over time the seasons will change, trees, plants, leaves will grow and die – only to come to life again in the spring. Seasons will come and go. The sun will set, the day will end and things have already changed. These kinds of changes we are used to – because they happen everyday – we see them constantly and have grown used to them. Your life will also change as each day passes. In some cases there will be changes that you want, changes that you feel you don't want and unexpected changes – but there will be change. If you don't embrace these changes – if you don't accept them and make them a part of your life – you fail to use the Power of Change and you cripple your ability to create the life that you want. In the end you paralyze your subconscious mind and you suffer unnecessarily, you get hurt, depressed, angry and resentful – and it's only because you didn't embrace change – you didn't work with the Power Of Change.

Think of change as opportunity – change always brings with it an opportunity to go in a different direction in life. Those who take advantage of that opportunity and follow up will reap the rewards. Those that resist and decide to stay where they are only because it is comfortable – will never advance – after all, they've chosen to stay where they are so there is really no possibility for advancing.

The process of life involves change and if you can recognize change, embrace change, and make adjustments to your life when change happens you will ultimately enjoy the most rewarding and successful life.

Now think about this: would you like to achieve all your goals? Would you like to be the person who gets what they want, enjoys life, has time to spare and is completely fulfilled? Most of us would love to have that kind of life – but are you committed and dedicated to making it happen? If not – then nothing will ever get better. Why not? Because in order for those things to happen – in order for you to achieve your goals and live the life you want – things have to change. And before things can change – you have to make a commitment to allow change to happen and you also have to agree to make some major changes in yourself, this includes changing the way you see things, the way you deal with people, the way you conduct your life, the way you think and what you believe. Creating Change is not just about hoping and praying, it's about doing, and being ready to embrace change when it arrives.

If you want to improve your life, if you want to achieve your goals you first need to make a solid commitment to change or improve things. Don't take this lightly – because your commitment is the foundation for change and a better life. Too often I hear people say; "Oh yeah, I'm going to make a commitment – I definitely want to change – in fact, as of tomorrow I'm going to make a list and get started." Then tomorrow comes and nothing changes. Instead, they get distracted and forget about the so-called commitment they made. A week later here's what they'll say: "You know I meant to get started last week but I just got too busy. Something came up – I can't remember what – but this week I'm definitely going to get started." The week comes and goes and nothing changes. There were too many things that came up. Hey – everyday there are things that come up and if you don't stay focused those "things" will throw you off track and in the end nothing gets done. Nothing improves because you were too busy being distracted. Everything around you will change – the time, date and year will change but the quality of your life will not improve because you did not make a commitment to change and you did not embrace change. In short – you did not agree to utilize the Power Of change.

A commitment to improve your life means you are going to do everything you can to make sure things get better. It says that you are going to take action and start by focusing on what you need to do to create the changes you want. If you don't stick to that commitment you'll only get distracted. If you keep that commitment at the forefront of your mind – then when you sense something coming that could distract you – you'll take charge and make the time to create the change you want.

When you have this commitment in place and when you say that you are ready to embrace change – that you understand that there is something good in all changes, that any change allows you to grow and move in a new direction, that change helps you move closer to achieving the goals that you are now focused on – then your subconscious mind picks up this message. It then begins working with the power within the universe to bring about the events, situations, people and circumstances that will lead to the changes needed for you to achieve your goals. Your subconscious mind says: "hey, you're ready for change – let's get to work and make it happen." This only happens when you make a commitment to change and when you are ready to embrace change.

This process is another key component in the Power of Believing and it is another technique that I have my students practice on a regular basis when they work with my Creating Power system.

If you're in debt and you want to get out of it – then make a commitment – and start by not taking on any more debt. If you want to be in a relationship – then start by making it a priority to go out and meet people. If you want to get a job – then make a commitment to create the change you want and follow up by going out and doing everything you can to get a job and keep going until you get things done.

Now understand that when you make that commitment – there will be changes that come with it – but those changes will only happen if you stick to your commitment and do everything you can to achieve your goal. If you are committed to having the right relationship – understand that your life will change when you meet and be with the right person. You will have to deal with another person, you will have to share your time, your love, possibly your home and finances, you will have to make time for the other person, you will have to be understanding, supportive and dedicated.

If you want to get out of debt then understand that there will be changes. In this case you won't be able to spend as much as you once did, you'll have to take better control of your money, you'll have to be more responsible with what you buy and where you spend your money, you'll have to cutback in some areas until you get out of debt. If you want to get a new job there will be changes as well. You will have to be at work at a certain time, you'll have to get to know new colleagues, you'll have to learn how the new company operates, you'll have to make new friends and deal with the politics of any job, you'll have to learn how to get along with your new boss or bosses, and you'll have to be a dedicated employee.

Don't take the changes lightly – you have to be ready for them because they will happen once you make that commitment and when they happen, if you're not ready – you could end up throwing away a tremendous opportunity to achieve your goals.

So the first thing I want you to do is to make a commitment to create change in your life – it's a commitment to improve or significantly change certain aspects of your life. You can fill out the following form or write out the agreement I've outlined on a separate piece of paper:

I, (insert your name here)_____ hereby promise to accept change and drastically improve my life. From this day (insert date) _____ I will embrace change and begin improving my life dramatically.

Signed_____.

I know some of you will feel the above exercise is unnecessary – but the point of the exercise is to imprint on your brain and subconscious mind that you are ready to accept change and drastically improve your life.

Now that you've completed that step let's move on to the second important aspect of this chapter and that involves a decision. You must now decide exactly what it is you want to change, why you want those things to change and then think about what you can do to make those changes happen. Notice: – I said what you CAN do – not what you HAVE to do. You really don't have to do anything. Just start by doing what you can and keep adding to the lists of things that you can do whenever you want. After a while you'll realize that you can do anything – even though you don't have to, you'll actually want to – and it will actually be enjoyable because you'll start seeing results. What exactly do I mean? Creating Change is a process and you build on each step as you go. So at first it may not seem like you're making a lot of progress – but as you continue to do something everyday towards changing certain aspects of your life or achieving a particular goal – you'll see things start to improve. If you don't see improvements – then make adjustments as you go. For example: let's say you want to get a job. The real goal is not always to get a job – you want to get a job for a number of different reasons one of them may be to make some money, or to increase your earnings.

So what you really want to change is your earnings – you want to improve the amount of money that you make. Getting a job is just one way of making money – but there are plenty of other ways to make money. Now everyday begin thinking of what you can do to make some money – do something everyday that will help you make more money; you could look for a job, explore a business venture, turn a hobby into a moneymaking possibility, start a business with a friend, get a part-time job, go back to school to learn a new skill, the list goes on – but if you're only thinking about getting a job your turning away other opportunities. If you're not getting results by getting a job from searching through the want ads, adjust course and try something different.

Refine your goal, re-examine what you want to change and be open to all possibilities.

Some of you may be asking: "Hey Karim, what's all this got to do with the Power Of Believing." The answer is quite simple. If you want changes to happen in your life, and if you want these changes to significantly improve your life – then you have to believe that change is for the better. If you want change, embrace change; you may be ready for change – but if you don't believe that change will happen and that it will be for the better – you won't see the opportunities when they arrive because you'll be too busy believing that change is not for the better.

Here's an example: If you wanted to settle down and have children but ended up breaking up with your boyfriend/girlfriend would you consider that change a setback? Or would you believe that the change is for the good and look at the possible, positive outcomes? I would contend that if you want to get married, settle down and have children and you are now single again because you broke up with your girlfriend/boyfriend – you now have the opportunity to attract and be with the right person – the person who shares your vision of having a family. The breakup is actually an opportunity to meet someone terrific but you will only be able to recognize this opportunity when you believe that all change is good and essential to your growth, even the breakup that you just endured.

The power of believing lies in what you believe – if you believe that change is difficult and not always good – then you will attract situations that will make you feel that way. But if you believe that change is always good – then you will always attract situations that make you feel that change is good – because you will always experience positive outcomes.

You have your exercises for this chapter; make a commitment to embrace and accept change. Make a commitment to create changes. Make Creating change a priority; learn to work with the power of change by always looking for new opportunities and positive outcomes when change arrives. Think about what you want, understand how achieving that goal will change your life and accept that those changes are for the better so that you can embrace change.

I know a lot of people have a challenging time when it comes to change. But I too have been through a great deal of changes in my life. I started my journey in East Africa and have lived in a number of different cities – always dealing with change. It isn't until you embrace change that good things really begin to happen.

Here's a personal example: Shortly after 9-11 in 2001, I found that many things around me were changing. My father had passed away, my friends had left New York, my mother was getting older and not very comfortable being on her own and I was getting older. I was no longer the brash kid – I was all grown up covering the biggest story in the world and there was change all around me. I knew that my life was going to drastically change – but I didn't know exactly how. You might ask how I knew this. When I see things changing around me, when I see the lives of my friends changing and my family being impacted by change – I know my turn is not too far in the distance. I look at those signals as intuitive messages coming from the universe. Before my father passed away I had promised him that I would take care of my mother – that she would be in good hands. But I lived in New York and she was in Toronto – as much as I tried I knew I wasn't fulfilling my commitment.

So in the Spring of 2002 I went back to Toronto – just to visit and consider setting up an office where my mother could help out with some of the business of Creating Power and my other projects. We had also developed a growing list of overseas and Canadian clients and thought she would be able to help a great deal in this area. I spent the summer in Toronto then went back to New York. Later in the Year I was back in Toronto and this time I seemed to stay longer than I expected. Before I knew it I was getting involved in charities, playing soccer with new friends, getting caught up with old friends. Spring came and I was still there –

and before I could pack my bags I had met a wonderful woman and fallen in love. The rest is history.

I still have my place in New York – but I spend a great deal of my time in Toronto. When my father was alive a friend once asked if I would ever move back to Toronto – at the time I didn't think I would – but things changed and I know the only reason why I had such good fortune was because I embraced that change and allowed myself to explore new opportunities when they arrived. Sure we could have handled the overseas clients from New York, but my mother didn't like living in New York – her home was Toronto and she is a big part of my life and this company – after all she taught me everything I teach you today. So her happiness was important – I just didn't expect that following the path of change would lead to such good fortune for me.

I think you get my point. Be open to change, embrace it, and explore the wonderful possibilities and opportunities that arrive – then you will begin creating the life you truly want.

Question:

"Karim, I know that I need to change, I know I need to become a better person, focus on my goals and I know that all of this has to be done soon. I've been a very negative person for as long as I

can remember and now my husband has had enough. If I don't shape up he says he's going to leave. I just can't seem to change. Can you help, please!"
-Norma. T

Answer:

Hi Norma,

Right now your mind is used to being negative and doesn't even know how to begin being positive. The only way to get it to change and go in a new direction is to start by training your mind to become positive. To do this you have to first start by looking at the positive situation in every event that takes place. This will be awkward at times and you will likely have to force yourself to find positive situations in every event – but it will help you get started. Next – work with the techniques that I've outlined because they will also help train your mind to become more positive. Now that you know you have to change you have to make a commitment to change – are you ready for it? Do you want to change? Or do you want to go on being negative and drive your husband and others away from you? I think we know the answer – now it's time to make a commitment to change and to help you along I suggest you look at all the benefits that will come from changing. Think about all of the good things that would happen and how your life would improve. Then ask yourself if changing is worth it? If it is – then you have your motivation – you know why you want to change. Then the process will focus on changing the way your mind works but you will be able to do this if you stick with many of the exercises I've outlined and remember why changing is so important. Good luck.

Question:

"Every time I think about my goals I first get excited, then after I get started on them I get nervous and start to get scared. I'm scared that people won't like me if I change, I'm scared that I won't be able to handle change, I'm scared that when I succeed I won't like who I am. What should I do?"
-Darren S.

Answer:

Hi Darren,
Thanks for writing. I want you to think about a couple of things and then see what you come up with. When you experience fear it's usually a sign that you're not prepared for what is ahead. In your case it sounds like you're not prepared for the changes that will come when you accomplish your goals. While you have to make a commitment to change – you should also make a commitment to stay true to yourself. Who says you have to change when you accomplish your goals? If you seriously think that people won't like you when you accomplish your goals then ask yourself why not? See what answers you come up with. Remember –

you get to decide who you want to be and if you decide that you don't want to change – then you don't have to change when you accomplish your goals. Once you prepare yourself for the changes by deciding who you want to be when you accomplish your goals you'll be better prepared and you'll be ready to create the changes you want.

Question:

"I'm tired of things the way they are. I want more out of life, I know I can do more but I don't know how. What should I do?"
-Angela.

Answer:

Angela it's great that you want things to change, it's great that you know you can do more and that you can have a better life – now you have to decide what it is that you want. Take some time to yourself and think about what kind of life you want and how you want things to unfold over the next five years, ten years and 20 years. You've made your commitment to change – now decide what it is you want to change. Once you do that you can focus on training your mind and directing your subconscious mind to help you achieve your goals. You can also begin taking the steps you need to take in order to create the life you want. The sooner you get started the sooner you'll achieve the changes you want.

Question:

"Karim, I hope you read this. I'm in a relationship and I can't take it anymore but I also can't bear the thought of having to break up and go through all those emotions again. My boyfriend is very negative, puts me down all the time, he doesn't want to change. How can I change him?"
-Sunita.

Answer:

Sunita, it seems like there is a lot going on and the first thing you should accept, although I know it's not what you want to hear, is that you cannot change your boyfriend. In fact, you likely cannot change anybody, except yourself. Your boyfriend has his own mind and his own subconscious mind and will decide what he wants. While you can work on being positive and finding ways to improve the relationship you won't be able to change him. You may be able to get him to see things differently, you may be able to help him grow and develop respect – but you won't outright change him. So you have to decide if you want to stay and work things out – knowing you may be able to improve your relationship but won't be able to change your boyfriend or do you want to move on? Breakups are always a difficult thing mainly because there are so many emotions involved, but change is always good. Deep down inside you know what you have to do to enjoy the life you want and if you're not sure – start focusing on making the right decision.

You don't have to know what that decision is right now — but if you focus on making the right decision, if you tell yourself that you are making the right decision you'll be guided to making the right decision. Deep down inside you know what is best — you just have to uncover that answer. And by working with the techniques I've outlined here and in my Creating Power system you'll be able to uncover those answers.

creatingpower.com

4

Power Of Believing

"The mind is the limit. As long as the mind can envision the fact that you can do something, you can do it - as long as you really believe 100 percent."
- Arnold Schwarzenegger

At the very beginning of this book I explained how incorporating the Power of Believing helps you achieve all your goals and allows you to live the life that you want. So far you've gone through some technical steps – which involved understanding what you want and why, setting goals, and coming up with a plan to achieve those goals, and you also learned how to focus on your goals and the importance of not stressing, worrying or obsessing over your goals. Now comes the not so technical aspect – this is the part that may be difficult for those who are used to seeing things in black and white – or those who always follow the principle that seeing is believing. In order to truly enjoy success and happiness you will have to develop a level of trust between yourself and your subconscious mind, and between yourself and the universe. Instead of following the principle that seeing is believing – you may want to reverse that so that you follow a new philosophy that now says believing is seeing.

The Power of Believing lies in your ability to trust that you will get what you ask for, you will get what you deserve and that you deserve what you ask for while accepting that what you desire may not come in a way which you planned but that it will happen – in time. The last 2 words always seem to cause people to give up because while most will invest all of the effort – only the truly successful people will invest the time. You may feel that you don't have time and that things have to happen for you right now, that changes must come immediately and at once. Sorry – but that's not the way it works. I explained at the very start of this book that things won't happen overnight, that they can happen overnight – but more than likely you have to give yourself, your subconscious mind and the universe some time to help you create the changes you want in life.

Try to look at it this way – you're sailing on this giant Cruise ship called "Your Life" and you're the Captain. Suddenly one day you realize you're going the wrong way – in fact you're going in the complete opposite direction. But this giant ship has this momentum and it just keeps going even though you've shut down all of the engines – you're not coming to a grinding halt. You then realize that you have to start turning this ship around – otherwise you're doomed. Do you think you'll be able to turn the ship around in a minute? 5 minutes? 10-minutes? And what if you did turn it around – you'd have to head back in the direction you came from until you got back on the right course and then you would finally be heading in the right direction. If you had been sailing in the wrong direction for 10 days how long do you think it would take for you to backtrack and get on the right course? Now what if you had been on the wrong course for 15-years?

You may feel that you're on the wrong course right now, and that you've been heading in the wrong direction or the direction you don't want for quite some time, now you want that to change. You're not going to get on track right away. You're going to have to turn things around slowly – just like turning around that cruise ship, and you're going to have to go in a different direction. This will all happen one-step at a time.

To develop the power of believing you should look at your goals as a long-term objective with the understanding that everything you do on a daily basis allows you to become better at developing and utilizing the Power Of Believing. As each day passes you move closer towards achieving your goals because you are doing all of the other exercises I outlined in this book. As you continue working with those exercises you track your progress and you see how things start to develop and unfold for you.

In order to begin applying the Power Of Believing you should simply trust that you are being guided every step of the way. You should learn to develop this trust with your subconscious mind and the universe and to help you do this I suggest you start small – by working with some smaller goals. By doing this you give yourself a chance to begin achieving small goals and then build on them for encouragement. It's just like training for that marathon that I referred to earlier in this book – in that case you wouldn't expect to go out and run 20+ miles your first time out especially if you had never run before. I know some of you might think about doing just that and if you had expectations of running a marathon in record time your first time out, you're only setting yourself up for disappointment and a rude awakening. When you're in training you set your target and then start building towards that goal. When you apply the same process in life you increase your chances for success.

Every professional athlete started at an amateur level and they built on their success by continually training and aiming for a specific target. Consider this a similar process that you've begun in this book, now your in basic training and as you begin to achieve some of your smaller goals you begin to believe in yourself, you begin to believe that you can achieve some goals and that you can accomplish something. Soon after you'll begin to believe that you can achieve your ultimate goal.

I had a student named André, who wanted to make a million dollars and when I first started working with André he wanted to make that million in 6 months. At the time André was working for a trucking company – mainly taking care of scheduling and handling the drivers. When ever he had some extra time André would get involved in sales – trying to sign on new clients for large, cross-country deliveries. When we first started working together André had no idea how to go about making a million dollars – his current salary paid him 35-thousand dollars a year and if he had a good year in sales he would make an extra 20-thosuand dollars. He soon realized that 35-thousand dollars a year was a long way from a million.

The first thing we did was break down how long it would take him to make a million dollars if he just worked at his current job. When he found out it would take about 20-years André soon realized that working in the trucking industry wasn't going to get him to a million dollars anytime soon – at least not doing what he was doing. I explained to André that he had to give himself a realistic time frame – one where he could come up with a new plan and a new way to make a million dollars.

The first few weeks were quite the challenge. André was ready to give up on many occasions. He had gone from wanting to make a million dollars to just trying to make sure he could pay his bills. But at the end of the day he always realized that simply being able to pay the bills just wasn't good enough. I explained to André that while his long-term goal was to make a million dollars – his first goal should be to simply increase his revenue – he should just try to make a little bit more money. André's immediate reaction was that he could do this by improving his sales ability – and he did. Within a few weeks he had made an additional 7-thousand dollars. After continuing to do this he realized that a lot of the companies liked him and were willing to give him business. Now André started to believe in himself – he started to believe that he could make more money and that maybe he could even make a million dollars. I recall numerous phone conversations where André always asked me: "Karim, this is great, I'm making more money but how am I going to make a million dollars." My answer was simple: "Keep doing what you're doing, and just keep believing that soon you'll find a way to make a million dollars. Focus on finding a way to make a million dollars, believe that there is a way to make a million dollars and you'll find a way to make a million dollars. Don't stress out over it – just do your job and trust that you will find a way."

André would sometimes grow frustrated, while he was making more money he still hadn't made a million and he still hadn't found a way to make a million dollars – and he had only been working with my Creating Power system and some of the techniques I've outlined in this book for 4-months. During his 5th month something interesting and exciting happened. André took a day off to go sailing with one of the clients he had recently signed. André didn't love sailing but figured he liked the water and this would be a terrific break. He called me later that evening with some exciting news. The client he was with wanted to open up a new distribution company and felt André had the expertise to get things to certain places on time and he had been impressed by André's work ethic. After going back and forth for a few months André and his client worked out a deal where André would be a minority partner in the new company, would receive shares in the company, a bonus, a salary, incentives and would be a Vice President in the company. His average yearly salary would net him close to 300-thousand dollars a year. Not quite a million right? Not so fast. After a year of running the company André realized that his shares alone were valued at a million – it didn't happen in 6-months – but it did happen. For André waiting a year and a few months was worth every penny.

André's success came about because he learned to work with and apply a number of different techniques which he got from my Creating Power system – but he managed to put it all together because he started to believe that he could make more money and that belief came about because he found a way to make more money and continued to build on it. André was also doing something he enjoyed – it was a new challenge and he was having fun learning and making more money. André was able to go from making a few thousand dollars more a month to making millions because he believed there was a way to make that leap – he just had to find it. He also followed up on opportunities, took the time and made the effort to be nicer to his new clients and he also took the day off to go have some fun – which is when he really made his millions.

Now you could apply his formula and you may not have the same success. Why not? Because if you apply the power of believing superficially – just so that you can accomplish something without truly believing or without truly working with the process – you are actually trying to trick your subconscious mind and cheat the process – this never works. I can give you countless stories of people who have said they do all the work, claim they believe and are open to new possibilities but when I get them on the phone and ask them the tough questions I find out that they are filled with doubt, they don't believe but are actually trying to say that they believe so that they can hurry up and accomplish their goals. This attempt at trying to trick yourself or cheat the process doesn't work and will only set you back further.

I know there are some who will tell you: "simply believe and you will achieve everything." This is true – but as I said at the very beginning of this book – it is often challenging to believe that everything will get better when you look around you and you don't see much hope. By focusing on what you want, by setting your long-term goal, by following up and breaking your long-term goal into smaller goals, by trusting that there is a way to achieve your goals, by working to find a way to achieve your goals you begin to take small steps to help you create the life you want, you begin to believe that you can achieve your long-term goals because you begin to make progress – but this will only happen if you focus on the progress that you are making and not focus on what is wrong.

There comes a point in this process where you must trust that your subconscious mind, and the powers of the universe will guide you and help you achieve your goals. Sometimes before you get there you have to endure a number of ups and downs. Some people suggest that these are tests – to see if you truly do believe. I don't consider them tests – instead they are just a result of your long-time negative thinking process that has dominated your life for so long. Your current situation is anchored by your thoughts of the past. Your thoughts today create your future; your beliefs today create your future. There is a time lag between when your old thoughts and old beliefs run out and your new thoughts and your new beliefs take over. You are now in the process of changing your beliefs – and thus changing your future. Your present state is simply a result of your past thoughts and past beliefs. There is no test – it's just you who has created all those challenges that you run into. But the good news is that after a while – your new thoughts and new beliefs will take over and those challenges will fade away.

Let me give you another example of how trying to cheat the process never works and that only when you start to truly believe do you unleash the Power of Believing – and that's when you get results.

A few years ago I had a client, whom we'll call Dianne, who wanted to meet her soul mate. She was 34 years old, living in Dallas, Texas and was very tired of the dating scene. She had been in plenty of relationships, had even been proposed to by 2 different men, once when she was 24 and again when she was 29 – both times she believed she was too young. She had other things she wanted to do – important things like traveling and focusing on her career. She also didn't think the men were right for her and felt she needed to be with someone more compatible. When she first started working with my Creating Power system she discovered that when it came to men and relationships she had been attracting everything that she believed. She believed men were difficult, complicated, overbearing, and stubborn and so she always ended up with men who had those characteristics. She also believed that it was difficult to find good men, that there were no good men out there and that the dating scene was a waste of time. She felt that her friends didn't know anybody worthy of her dating so she didn't see any point in talking to her friends about meeting someone – because she believed that they didn't know anybody.

You can see that there is quite a stream of negative thinking and a strong, negative belief system about relationships and men. Naturally she was having a tough time finding Mr. Right – especially since she didn't believe he existed. One day I simply asked her: "Dianne, Would you look for a 50-dollar bill in your backyard if you didn't think it existed?" Her answer was no. I then asked her: "Then why are you looking for somebody you don't believe exists?" There was silence over the phone and then she said: "So I guess I'm wasting my time huh?" I explained that she was wasting her time if she believed that Mr. Right didn't exist – because she would never attract him or meet him. But I then explained that if she simply changed her belief system – that if she really started to believe that he did exist – she would meet him.

We talked about this for some time and I explained that in order to create a new, positive belief system that would allow her to attract the right person she should look at all the reasons why such a man would exist. Dianne had to look at all the possible ways she could meet a man, think of all the men that exist in the entire world and that of the billions of single men – there was really a high probability that she could meet one that would knock her off her feet. She agreed to start working on her belief system. Two days later she called and said: "Karim, you know – I'm starting to get this – I really believe that I can meet this person. I'm starting to feel better already – I just know I'm gonna meet this guy."

A couple of weeks passed and Dianne called again – she had been on a date that didn't go very well – he simply wasn't Mr. Right. I explained that there is a process at work and that just because you didn't meet the right person on your very first attempt doesn't mean the process isn't working. We talked further and she explained that in the week before the date she had a relapse – where she only focused on how wrong things were in her life, she thought about all the bad dates, and how difficult it was to meet men. She also believed that this man would not be a good candidate – after all so far no one had been a good candidate and sure enough – things didn't go well. But she said: "I still believe

Karim, I still believe I'm gonna meet this guy." I then told Dianne that she really didn't believe. She wanted to believe – but she really didn't believe. I explained that if she really did she wouldn't have been thinking about all the things that had gone wrong in her love life. If she really did believe – she wouldn't even worry about whether this was the right guy or not. If she really believed – she would have gone on the date, made the most of it – and trusted that her subconscious mind, the Universe and the Power of Believing were all at work guiding her in the right direction. The date may have been a way for her to fine tune what she wanted in a man and what she didn't want in a man, it may have been a way for her to help someone along in their journey and help them discover their own path, the person she met may have turned out to be a good friend or a valuable acquaintance in the future. When you truly believe – you trust that things are working in your favor and that you are being guided in the process so that you make the right decisions by meeting the right people at the right time and by being at the right place so that you can embrace the opportunity. Dianne did none of that. But I am happy to say that after working with Dianne for a few months she was able to turn the corner and after a year of completing the Creating Power system she met Mr. Right. They got married in 2000 and had their first child in 2002. It took some time for her to understand and apply the Power Of

Believing, but when she did she started getting results.

You can't cheat the process – you can't cheat the Power of Believing. I hear from a lot of people who say they believe but really don't believe. Now they are not intentionally trying to cheat or manipulate the process – it's just that they don't know how the process works. Most people want to believe, they will try to convince themselves that they do believe if they feel it will help them achieve their goals. They try to convince me all the time that they believe when they really don't. There is no use trying to convince yourself of something that isn't true especially when you know it won't help you. Take a look at your belief system; break it down into smaller everyday beliefs – the kind of beliefs that are backed with statements you often don't even think about. Then see if you truly believe that you can achieve your goals and live the life you want.

If you find that you have limiting beliefs – start changing them by working with some of the techniques I've outlined. In addition to those techniques – look at why you can achieve something and instead of coming up with a list of reasons of why you can't. Yes, you will have legitimate reasons for not being able to do something – and that's okay. All I'm suggesting is that you look at why and how you can do something. By doing this you start to realize that you can accomplish your goal and because you feel you have reasons for why things can work out.

The Power of Believing is one of your greatest assets – if you begin to believe that you truly can accomplish something. It all starts with taking small steps, which leads to taking big steps – but you have to start the process.

Here's an example of the level of belief that you need to have in order to accomplish your goal. When you go to bed at night – do you believe that you will wake up in the morning? Most of you have a firm conviction that you will wake up in the morning. That's the level of belief you need to have in order to utilize the power of believing. You have to have a firm conviction that you deserve to accomplish your goals; that you can and will accomplish all your goals because it is your right and responsibility to live a better, comfortable life. When you have that level of conviction you begin to utilize the power of believing.

I have one important story to share with you on the topic of believing and this is a true story about a much-celebrated athlete – some of you may not be old enough to have seen him compete, but you've likely heard of him. In 1974 Muhammad Ali was about to fight George Foreman for the heavyweight championship of the world – back then the title actually meant something. Foreman was a huge favorite and everybody, including Ali's trainers thought Ali would be destroyed in the ring. Everybody who was directly associated or involved with the fight believed Ali was going to lose – everybody except one person – that one person who believed Ali would win was Muhammad Ali. During the fight it looked like it was only a matter of time before Ali would get knocked out – until the 7th round when Ali came from nowhere and knocked out George Foreman. Ali was once again Champion of the World.

Only you need to believe in yourself. Only you need to believe that things will improve and that your life is getting better. What others say and do should not concern you – in order for the Power Of Believing to work you and only you need to work with and apply it.

Question:
I've tried much of what you say and in the past I have believed but nothing materialized. In fact things have become worse and now I find it very hard to believe anything you or anybody else tells me.
-Disappointed.

Answer:
Hi there,
I'm sorry that things didn't workout in the past. I

would like to know exactly what you did and what you believed. Often we tell ourselves that we believe that things will get better – but you really don't have a full conviction that life will improve. You may have also been focusing on the wrong things or for the wrong reasons. Finally, you shouldn't believe anything I or anyone else tells you. The only person you need to believe in is yourself – work with the process and the power of believing, test it yourself – see if it works – be your own judge. I've never seen it fail and I know if you apply it correctly it will work for you as well.

Question:
How long should one wait before seeing results?
Patricia S.

Answer:
Hi Patricia,

If you had a newborn baby how long would you wait for it to start walking? Would you give it a week, 2 weeks, a month, five months, a year and then give up if the child didn't walk? Chances are you would be like most people – you simply believe the child will walk when it is ready. Doctors will give you time frames – but deep down inside you know the child will walk – you simply believe it. Too often we place artificial time limits on nature and the process of creating the life we want. But nature and your higher self have no concept of time – the measuring of time is something that we invented.

When you work with the Power of Believing you just know and believe that you will get results – time becomes irrelevant – it happens when you are ready. I know that's not what you want to hear – but it is the truth. It's not about waiting because results are always taking place and finally – the results you see will vary from student to student. It really depends on your goals, where you are now, what you want to achieve, how old you are, how much change has to take place, how many beliefs have to change and how often you work with the exercises. Someone who works with the exercises once a week is not likely to see dramatic results. Someone who works with the exercises daily and regularly will likely see results sooner.

Question:
"I believe with all my heart that my boyfriend will come back to me. It's been 2 years and I have not heard one word from him – not even a phone call nothing. I still believe that he will come back but is there anything else that I can do."
-Clara.

Answer:
Hi Clara,
This is not how the Power of Believing works. You cannot control others or compel them to do something they may not want to do. I know that's not your direct intention – but while you may believe that your boyfriend will come back to you –

it's time to ask yourself why you believe that? By this I mean what is it that you really want? Do you want your boyfriend back or do you really want to experience love and the joys of relationship again? I would suggest that you focus on experiencing the love and joy of a relationship again – believing that you will meet the right person. If you're ex' is the right person then you two will re-connect. If he is not – then you will meet someone else who will fulfill your quest for love and a wonderful relationship. Believe in the result that you want – don't believe that you can make someone come back if they really don't want to – that likely will not happen. Focus on what you truly want – and then believe that you have it.

Question:

I want to say that your material has been truly helpful. My life has improved dramatically and your techniques really work. I have one question – how often should I work with these techniques? I find it hard to remember to do everything. Thank you Karim.
-Jennifer S.

Answer:

Hi Jennifer,

Thank you for writing – I'm so happy to see that you stuck with the *Creating Power course* and you're getting results. Now to answer your questions: the reason you forget to do some of the work is because your mind is not used to working with these techniques and is not used to applying them everyday. In short – it hasn't become a habit for you. So that means you should work with the exercises everyday, as often as you want, when ever you want and when ever you can. You might want to set up a routine so that you do some in the morning, another group in the afternoon, some more in the early evening and a final set at night. I would also suggest that you do some of the exercises while you're driving, walking, eating lunch – anytime that your mind is not actively engaged in something important is a good time to do the exercises I've outlined. By following this routine you'll create a habit and your mind will accept this new habit – once that happens you'll begin to see dramatic improvements in your results.

5

Power Of Open Mindedness

> "The real voyage of discovery consists not in making new landscapes but in having new eyes."
> - Marcel Proust

Every week I hear from potential students asking me about my Creating Power system and most of them tell me about how they want to achieve their goals and about how they often try but feel they're just not getting anywhere. They'll go into great details about how they have tried everything and still they're not getting any results. Often they've tried just about every course and want to know how I can help them. The amazing thing that I discover during my conversations with these potential students is that just about all of them have in fact had plenty of opportunities presented to them, opportunities that could have changed their lives – but they just didn't see them.

Instead, they closed their mind to the possibilities; their inability to see these opportunities prevented them from achieving their goals. How did this happen? It happens mainly because you are stubborn – perhaps not intentionally – but you feel that you should achieve your goals in a certain way and thus refuse to consider other possibilities. When you get stubborn, when you close your mind and limit yourself by saying things have to be done a certain way or that they have to happen in a certain way you greatly decrease the odds of your success and open the door to even greater failures.

If you kept an open mind and didn't limit yourself to the way you feel things should unfold and what the possibilities should be – you would stand a better chance of creating the life you want and you would likely achieve your goals a lot sooner. By keeping an open mind you would grow as a human being and experience success regularly. I know there are a lot of you who will say that you do have an open mind – or at least you think you do – but this isn't about convincing yourself – it's about practicing and in this chapter I'm going to outline why you need to keep an open mind, how to go about keeping an open mind, how not to limit your opportunities by closing your mind and how to recognize opportunities through keeping an open mind. It's about creating the ability to work with and utilize the Power Of Open-Mindedness, a power that will help you discover new opportunities and live a more fulfilling and rewarding life. Working with the other techniques I've outlined will help you attract opportunities, but utilizing the Power Of Open Mindedness will help you recognize those opportunities that will lead you to success and happiness.

The Importance Of Keeping an Open Mind

Why is it so important to keep an open mind? Why not be stubborn and stick to your guns – demanding that everything unfold the way you want and according to your schedule? – After all you should have what you want – right? Sure you can have what you want but when you have a closed mind you limit yourself to possibilities and chances are you'll miss a great deal of opportunities.

When you have an open mind you allow yourself to attract opportunities because by keeping an open mind you tell your subconscious mind and you tell your higher power – that part of you that wants to guide you through life and provide only what is best for you – that you are willing to experience new possibilities, grow as a human being and try different things. This message allows your subconscious mind and your higher power to guide you to what you want in the quickest, safest, and most lucrative way possible. When you close your mind you tell your higher power and your subconscious mind that you are no longer interested in what is best for you, that you do not care about achieving your goals in the safest, quickest and most lucrative way. Instead, when you are stubborn you tell your subconscious mind and your higher power that you only want things done a certain way. Now what if how you want things done would actually cause great harm to yourself and those around you? What if the way you want things to unfold would cost you more money, time and effort? Would you still want things to unfold your way and according to your schedule? Or would you prefer to achieve your goals in the quickest, safest and most lucrative way possible?

I think the choice is obvious – but just in case you're still not sure I'll give you two examples from 2 people that I know very well. One of them we'll call, Jonas, who followed my Creating Power system and the other – Paul, a good friend whom I think has tremendous potential but is just very stubborn. Let's take a look at Paul's situation.

Paul is a very talented person, great guitar player and terrific music composer. Paul has been playing in bands for the past 15-years – always playing smaller clubs hoping for a big break. The funny thing is – I think he's had the opportunities – he just hasn't seen them. Paul knows he's a great musician but feels – or I should say believes that the only way he is going to make it big is to be signed by a record label – nothing else will do. He's sent out demos, talked to people who know people who know other people who know a few other people in the business but still hasn't had the break he's been looking for. I've talked to him several times about this and I've even asked him if he would consider doing studio music – where he would play for a band on their album. "No way, it's either me and my band cutting my cd or nothing. I'm not playing backup." Would he consider going on tour with a band for a few months – just to get the experience and meet some more people? His answer: "I've got plenty of experience, I've been playing for 15 years – I've done plenty of live stuff – I don't need the experience."

Now here's where it gets interesting. About 8 years ago Paul was asked to do some studio music and the money was really good from what I recall. He turned it down because he wanted to focus on his music and felt that his best shot was doing his thing. A few years later the same band asked him to fill on a tour for a few months. Again he turned it down because he had too many club dates booked and wanted to focus on his own music. Just a year later another band asked him to do some studio work and even wanted him to write some music for them – again he turned it down saying he wanted to focus on his music.

Some of you may agree with Paul and say he has the right to do what he wants and he should stick to his guns. That's where we disagree and here's why. Paul wants to play music and would love nothing more than to have his own album with his own band. In the process of focusing on his goal he is presented with numerous opportunities that will help him as a musician. He may play in a studio with other musicians and in the process learn a great deal about music, meet someone who likes his stuff and would like to hear his band. He could be on tour and he could meet someone who could help him and his band tremendously. He may end up being a better solo performer and leave his band to do his own thing – who knows? But Paul continues to limit himself by keeping his mind closed and limiting himself to succeeding only on his terms and at his time. Sure he and his band could get signed to a record label – but he may have been able to accomplish that a lot sooner, a lot easier, made a lot more money, enjoyed some great experiences and grown tremendously if he would just be open to all possibilities.

I had another potential student – we'll call Brenda. She was living in Eastern Europe, was fluent in French and wanted to live in Paris but said she had no work and no money and no way of getting to Paris. Her goal was to live in Paris and she wanted a job working in Paris. After talking to her for a while I discovered that she had been offered jobs but not in Paris. I suggested she take the work so she could save up the money to go to Paris. "No! I must work in Paris." But she wasn't working anywhere and she refused to look at the possibility of getting a job to make the money to get to Paris.

This person was simply too stubborn to work with and the last time I spoke to her – which was just before writing this book – she was still living in Eastern Europe and still unemployed. What do you think would happen if she took a job and tried to save up some money? Perhaps anything could happen.

You don't know how the road will unfold – where you are today is likely quite different from where you were 10 or 20 years ago. When you set a goal – you have a result in mind and you begin pursuing it – how you achieve that goal is something you cannot determine – that aspect is something your subconscious and your higher power will determine – and it will be done in the best, safest and quickest way possible when you keep an open mind.

A classic example of this process is Nelson Mandela – a man who set out to change the political climate of South Africa when he was a young man. His goal was to end apartheid and as an adult he did everything he could – include end up in jail for 26-years. But those 26-years didn't break him – he kept an open mind – always learning what he could, always speaking out through his representatives, always listening to people who would help him get out and end apartheid. Mandela accomplished his goal – his process required that he spend 26-years in jail and his incarceration ended when he realized that the only way he could get out and end apartheid was to strike a deal with the leaders of South Africa. After he did that he was freed and later became President and ended apartheid.

Another story that I like is that of NFL Quarterback Kurt Warner. Here is a football player who came out of college and was not picked to play professionally in the NFL. Instead, Warner played in the much smaller Arena Football League and World Football League. Eventually someone spotted him and realized he had talent. Warner went on to play for the St. Louis Rams, where he led them to the World Championship and was voted the league's Most Valuable Player – twice. Warner kept an open mind by playing in the smaller leagues – and that's where he got his break.

I said I would tell you about one of my students, Jonas who started working with my program when he wanted to get into basketball. Jonas was a good college basketball player – but wasn't drafted. He had talent – but he also knew the game very well. A few years had passed since his last college game and he was playing in Europe where he wasn't too happy because he had realized that he wanted to be back in the US. Jonas wasn't sure if he wanted to play professionally – it was once a dream but he was starting to realize a professional basketball player didn't always have a long career and an injury could end things very quickly, besides he was already a few years older and time wasn't going to be on his side for too long. But while playing in Europe Jonas also realized that he really loved being behind the scenes – studying games and going over game plans. A few months after working with my Creating Power system Jonas was offered a job as an assistant coach with a small college team in the United States. He thought about it and took the job. Three years later he was offered another job – this time as an assistant coach with a professional team. Jonas took the job and has never looked back.

Now during the course of working with Jonas there were many times when he wanted to experience the thrill of being a professional basketball player playing in his hometown. But he was open minded – and was willing to explore new possibilities. I talked to him just before writing this book and he said he has never looked back and that while he's happy being an assistant coach – he's open to other possibilities – including being a head coach or doing something completely different. Hey, you never know.

Keeping an open mind means that you are open to all possibilities – even if that means trying a different road or taking a different route to get to where you want to be. This means that you don't say – "Oh that's not for me. There can't be anything good in that." Or "Why would I want to do that? That's not what I was looking for." Or "I won't even consider that." Hey, let's remember one important factor – you don't know everything – and you don't always know what will or won't work out for you. If you never try something you'll never know whether you like it or if it will work out for you – and thus you can't say if it is right for you or not before even exploring the opportunity further. Only by keeping an open mind will you begin to explore all possibilities – and only by exploring all possibilities will you be able to determine which one is right for you and get on the right track so that you accomplish your goals.

Now I'm not talking about trying everything under the sun – but when you work with the power of your mind and subconscious mind as I've outlined here and as I've outlined in my *Creating Power course* – you begin to attract new opportunities. On the surface some of these opportunities may not seem like what you want but the only way to truly find out is to take a closer look and examine them.

Here's a personal example. Earlier, at the beginning of this book, I told you about how I had to get enough money to get to complete my Graduate Degree at NYU. Here's what happened. I was between semesters and looking for work when I was offered a job as an intern at the Sports division of CBC Radio in Toronto. I knew I had to come up with enough money to pay for my next semester's tuition and housing – not to mention the debt I had incurred from the first semester. The internship didn't pay much and I had another offer from another station, that paid a little better – but the job didn't start for a few weeks and was as a freelancer with no guarantee of work everyday. I decided to explore the opportunity with the station that offered the internship – while it didn't pay much – it offered a tremendous experience, the people were very encouraging and it seemed like a good idea at the time – even though it didn't pay as much as I needed. I thought I'd work there until I found something else. During my second day as an intern one of the network's correspondents had a heart attack and would be out for a few months. At the same time there was a breaking story in Toronto and they didn't have a reporter to cover it. My boss sent me – and in the process launched my career as a Reporter. Within a week they bumped me to full Reporter status and suddenly I was making the money I needed to pay the next semester's tuition.

A couple of things were in play before all this happened. I had worked with the powers of my mind and subconscious mind as I have outlined in this book and which I get into more detail in my *Creating Power course*. When the opportunities presented themselves I recognized that I had asked for something and my subconscious had brought the opportunities – now I had to follow up and explore both situations, which I did. I used the very same techniques I outline to make the right decision and thus was able to capitalize on the opportunity – that's why things worked out.

Had I not followed up on the opportunities presented, had I instead been stubborn and insisted on getting a high paying job to only pay for my tuition and housing, I would have never picked the right opportunity. By keeping an open mind I was able to try something different, while working with the power of my mind and subconscious to make the right decision.

Some additional things happened during my time as an intern/reporter with that station. My boss and I got along pretty well and when I decided I wanted to move from radio to television he suggested I speak to his good friend over at the network's television News division. That friend turned out to be the Head of Network Television News – who later hired me as a Reporter. Good things happen when you're open to all possibilities.

I know some of you may say "Karim I need the job now I have to pay the bills and what I'm getting isn't what I need." You don't know where these opportunities will take you. Some of them will work and some of them won't be right – but you won't know if you don't keep an open mind and try something or at least look into it further. Don't ever assume that you know how things are going to turn out – you don't. When you work with the power of your mind and subconscious mind – you'll also be able to make the right decision. Part of keeping an open mind is to understand that something may be right and sometimes something may not be right – while fully understanding and accepting that you will make the right decision. If you focus on making the right decision when you investigate opportunities – you'll make the right decision. If you worry about making mistakes – you'll make mistakes. If you keep an open mind and trust that you will make the right decisions, that you are being guided and that things will work out – you'll achieve your goals and enjoy a life filled with success and happiness.

How A Closed Mind Limits
Your Chance For Success

When you close your mind you essentially become stubborn and become a victim of the ego mind – you end up having an attitude that goes something like this: "This is what I want and I want it now. I'm not willing to try or accept anything else." This kind of attitude shuts you off from the process of life and nature – which is about growing and experiencing new possibilities. Think about how many times you were resistant to trying something new only to eventually give in and discover that you really enjoyed the process? I'm sure it's happened countless times. Kids are a perfect example. At first they're resistant to trying new things and then when they do – their whole attitude changes.

When you close your mind and become stubborn you essentially tell yourself, your higher self, and the natural forces of the universe that you're not willing to go the extra mile – that you're not willing to grow and experience new things. If you are not willing to grow, experience new things and instead choose to be stubborn or closed minded then there can be no change and no progress in life and things will never improve – it's that simple.

I'm not asking you to try everything under the sun, I'm not asking you to compromise your ethics and values – those are very important. But keeping an open mind also means to look at things a little differently and to see what else may be out there.

I know of many people who refuse to keep an open mind – who refuse to examine opportunities when they are presented only to end up getting frustrated and angry – often saying: "Things just suck – nothing ever works for me and I can never get a break." You are always given new opportunities – and so called "breaks" but if you close your mind to them you'll never see these opportunities, you'll never see the "breaks" and here's the worst part – things will never change and they may get worse.

If you want change or if you want to improve certain aspects of your life then you have to keep an open mind. Students who work with my Creating Power system learn to train their mind and subconscious mind so that they attract and explore new opportunities. Throughout this book I have provided different ways for you to train your mind and subconscious mind and part of the process of creating new beliefs and re-directing your mind and subconscious mind begins by looking at things differently, so that you take a closer look at opportunities, so that you listen to what people suggest and so that you become more aware of what is being presented.

How To Recognize Opportunities

If you want to recognize opportunities first realize that when you put out a message – when you seek to change or improve aspects of your life you will be guided by your subconscious mind, the universe and your higher power. Often these opportunities will come to you in various forms – rarely do they just fall in your lap or slap you in the face. Instead you may get a suggestion from a friend, you may read about something in the paper, hear something on the radio, a family member may also make a suggestion, someone from the past may come into your life with an opportunity – examine all of them.

Be more alert – listen to what people say – pay more attention to what's going around you. Ask yourself questions like: Why is this happening at this particular time? Why did that person make that suggestion? Was I seeking something – and did they have something of value to offer? Remember it goes both ways – sometimes somebody may present you with an opportunity, sometimes you may present them with an opportunity – sometimes you may help each other. When you're open to possibilities you'll recognize them. This process requires a higher sense of awareness, which will only improve with practice.

I'll go back to my earlier example – when I got the job as an intern, which launched my career as a reporter. The idea of applying for the job came to me from a friend – who had just started working fulltime at the network. I remember examining the opportunity – looking at the credentials of my friend. Here was someone whom I trusted, who was experienced in this field and who had my interests at heart. When I looked at the messenger I trusted that the message might be very helpful – because the messenger was credible. This is very important in making decisions and following up on opportunities. Examine where the message is coming from. A neutral party, someone who has your interests in mind, or is it coming from a source you don't trust and are skeptical about. If you're still not sure you can instruct your subconscious mind to guide you. You can do this by simply saying: "I'm making the right decision." This is the art of focusing on what you want and not on what you don't want. Focus on what you want to happen and you'll attract it. Be open to all possibilities – because when you're open to all possibilities, then only can anything truly happen.

Here now are some questions from my subscribers and students on the topic of keeping an open mind and uncovering new possibilities:

Question:
"Everyday I walk by a company that I have always wanted to work for. I have applied there several times but I've always been told that they'll get back to me and I never hear from them. I even have friends who work there and tell me what a great place it is. They have even tried to help me – but I have had no luck so far. I keep telling myself that I have a job there – and for a year now nothing has happened. I have a good job where I am but something tells me that I should get a job there. What can I do to get a job at that company."
-Jeanette M.

Answer:
Hi Jeanette,
I first have to ask why do you want to work at this

particular company? You say you have a good job and it sounds like you want to work at this company because your friends tell you how great it is – but it may not be that great for you. You are where you are because that is where you need to be right now. If you want to get a better job or work at a better company then focus on that – let your subconscious mind and higher power guide you to the job that is right. You may end up at that particular company you may not – but you will end up with a better job at a better company if that's what you choose. You don't know if the company you want to work at is right for you – it may sound like it is – but you don't really know. Focus on what you want and understand why – then keep an open mind and you'll end up being at the right place.

Question:

"I broke up with my girlfriend 2 years ago and I have to say that I always thought we would get back together. But it's been 2 years now and I don't think we will be getting back. My problem is that every time I go out and try to meet someone new I keep thinking that we will get back. I can't get the thought out of my head. What should I do?"
-Anil.

Answer:

Anil, it sounds like you're ready to move on but still have hope that you will get back with your ex-girlfriend. That's okay – there's nothing wrong with hope. But on another level it sounds like your mind is not letting go of your ex' and wants you to try and make things go back to the way they were. That's also okay – the mind likes to stay where it is comfortable and it has become comfortable with the thought of your ex' coming back. But if you're ready to move on then it's time to get the mind to move forward so that your subconscious mind will attract the right person. You can start doing this by telling yourself that you are keeping an open mind – that you are going to go out and meet new people, that you are attracting the right person and if that person is your ex' then so be it – if not – then you'll meet the right person and enjoy a great relationship. When your mind goes back to your ex' coming back – simply tell yourself – that's okay – if she comes back we'll deal with it then, if she's the right one – we'll get back, if someone else is the right one – then you'll meet her and have a great relationship – just keep an open mind. Anil, doing this once or twice won't change things right away and your mind will continue to put up resistance. But if you do this every time your mind thinks of your ex' you will see things start to change sooner and your mind will soon stop focusing on your ex' and understand that the priority is to be with the right person – which is what you want and that right person can be anyone – including your ex'.

Question:

"Karim, I've always wanted to make a lot of money in my life. I have a business, which I have been running for ten years. It does fairly well but I know we can do more. I keep trying different promotions – but nothing seems to create the kind of money I want. Any advice on how to take this business to the next level would be greatly appreciated."
-Thomas.

Answer:

Thomas, it sounds like on one level you want to make a lot of money, but on another level you want to improve your business – try to look at these as 2 completely different goals. Improving your business is one goal and making a lot of money is another goal. It seems that you think the only way to make a lot of money is through your business. But that's really not true because there are many ways to make a lot of money and through your business is just one way. If you want to make a lot of money then make this a goal, focus on it, train your mind and subconscious mind to guide you to the opportunities that will allow you to make a lot of money and then be open to all possibilities. You may find a way to do this through your business or you could achieve the goal in a completely different way – who knows? But if you're open to any and all possibilities you will discover the best way to make the kind of money you want. Finally – you should get specific on this goal – decide how much money you want to make. A lot is not a good enough guidance for your subconscious mind. Give your subconscious a specific target to work towards. Then start creating a belief system that allows you to achieve that goal and allows your subconscious mind to get you there.

Question:
"I've been trying to be a successful actress for the past 5 years and to support myself I work as a freelance writer – often writing articles for magazines and doing some reviews for newspapers and sometimes a local television station. My real goal is to be an actor – but I never get the work that I want and my writing/reporting career seems to be doing fairly well. How can I get back to acting?"
-Anna J.

Answer:
Anna, I think it's great that you want to be an actress – but you have to get clear on your goal and understand why you want to be an actress. I also think that it's interesting that your career as a writer seems to be evolving and growing, try to enjoy the process? Yes you want to be an actress – but your desire to be a successful actress has led you into a career that seems to be working out – at least right now it is. Your work as a writer may lead to bigger and better things – it may even help you

become a successful actress. I'm not suggesting that you give up on the goal of being an actress – instead keep focusing on it – but also be open to new possibilities. Your freelance work may lead you to a great career as a writer or a reporter – or in the process you could land some great work as an actress. First understand why you want to be an actress, continue focusing on your goal, enjoy the process, make the most of your budding career as a writer and be open to all possibilities, explore all opportunities and see what happens.

Question:

"Karim, I want to start a business but I don't know what kind of business and I don't know where to start. I know why I want to start a business – but I just don't know what kind of business. Can you help?"
-Unknown

Answer:

Hi there,

It's great that you want to start a business and it's even better that you know why you want to start a business. You're already half way to success. Believe it or not figuring out what kind of business is the easy part – especially since you're open to all possibilities and not limiting yourself to just one type of business. The truth is you know exactly what kind of business you want – you have the answer now you just have to uncover it. I would suggest you think about the qualities you want this business to have. For example – would you like to have a store where you deal with customers? Do you want to be a wholesaler? Do you want to market directly to the consumer? Is there a particular niche that you enjoy? How many hours do you want to work? How many days a week? Do you want to work from home? How much money do you want to make? Start thinking about the answers to these questions – when you do you likely won't have answers for all of them, but as you keep thinking about these questions you'll start to get answers. Then focus on finding or starting the right kind of business. Examine opportunities as they are presented. Listen to what friends or family have to say, listen to what people say and suggest, and then examine the opportunities that you discover. Believe that you have found the right business and you will. This the process of getting your mind and subconscious mind to work for you – your responsibility now is to do all you can to find the right opportunity.

6

Power Of Now

Love the moment. Flowers grow out of dark moments. Therefore, each moment is vital. It affects the whole. Life is a succession of such moments and to live each, is to succeed.
- Corita Kent, Sister of the Immaculate Heart of Mary

I'm about to reveal something very special and if you follow what I outline in this chapter you'll begin tapping a very powerful side of yourself — a part that will allow you to dramatically speed up your results and your ability to create the life you want. Not only will you get results but you will also begin to enjoy life a great deal. This aspect is not about achieving goals or getting tangible results — it will help you get results — but it is a different process and a different approach from what I outlined earlier in this book.

I call it the Power Of Now and in order to reap the rewards of the Power Of Now you don't have to endure weeks or months of training. Why? Because you are already living in the Now — you already live in the present moment and this is where you can draw upon tremendous power and positive energy that will help you enjoy life to its fullest. Let's face it – we all live in the present moment but most people fail to utilize the power that exists when you are in the now.

So in this chapter I'll outline how the Power Of Now works, why you need to begin working with the Power Of Now and how to start utilizing this amazing power so that you constantly enjoy life. I'll also outline how not working with the Power of the present moment can really cause a great deal of suffering and heartache – sadly this is what most people usually end up doing without even realizing what they are doing.

Understanding The Power Of Now

Let's face it the only thing that exists at this particular moment is what is happening right now. The only moment that is happening right now is that of you reading this book and absorbing the information. In a few minutes you'll be in another moment – perhaps you'll put the book down and do something else – or you may continue reading. That is then but at this precise moment, right now nothing else exists and nothing else matters. The past does not exist – it's over with and should be nothing but a fading memory. You cannot go through a door and enter the past – it doesn't exist. You cannot walk outside your home, get into your car and drive to the past – because the past does not exist – those moments of the past are long gone. Unfortunately too many people try to hang on to the past by re-living the past in their minds – by keeping distant memories of what was but no longer is. While you have the memories – the physical aspects of the past no longer exist. Yes an old boyfriend or girlfriend is still alive – but the relationship, the connection, the intimacy you shared no longer exists. Sure the company you once worked for still exists, but your place there, your job, your relationship within those walls no longer exists – it's in the past and the past is not here – the only thing that exists is what is here now. In a moment – the moment has changed and your moments, your present, your now – is constantly changing. Each moment that passes no longer exists. Only the present moment is what exists – and this is where you should be at all times – because this is where your power is.

The future also does not exist – it simply hasn't happened yet. You may think about the future, you may dream about it, you may worry about it, you may agonize over the future – but what you are really doing is wasting a lot of energy – because the future does not exist and there is really no way to predict it. Unfortunately those who are not living in the past are more than likely living in the future – hoping for a better day or worrying about what the future may bring – but in physical form – the future does not exist.

Both the past and the future are merely concepts, which consist of thoughts and memories – they have no physical form, and you cannot experience them. The past cannot be experienced again and the future cannot be experienced until it arrives. The only thing that you can experience and the only thing that really exists right now is the very present moment that you live in and from this present moment you can draw tremendous power and utilize positive energy – the kind of power and energy that can change your life and allow you to achieve your goals.

Now you may say that you don't like the present moment – but that's only because you're thinking about what you feel the present should be. You're either allowing your ego to dominate your present moment, or you're focusing on mistakes of the past, or you're consumed with the future, in the process you're forgetting to live in the present moment. I know some of you may say: "Karim, right now I don't have a job and the bank is about to foreclose. Plus my wife/husband just left me and I'm stuck with 3 kids. My present is not exactly pleasant." If your present or current situation is not pleasant then you are comparing it to something else – you're probably thinking about what the now should be instead of dealing with what is going on. You are focusing on the fact that you don't have a job because you feel you should have a job. There's nothing wrong with that – but look at what you have and think about what you can do – don't focus on what you don't have because you'll only attract more of what you don't want. In the above case if you don't have a job and you continually focus on the fact that you don't have a job you'll only create a life where you don't have a job, because you'll only attract what you don't want when you focus on it.

Now at this present moment you don't have a job – but at this present moment you feel you should have a job or have some way of making money. Then focus your attention on doing what needs to be done – which is to get a job or find a way to make some money so that you can pay the bills. So in this case you would start looking for work, you would focus on finding new ways to make more money. I'm not suggesting that you ignore the fact that you don't have work – focus on doing what you can to get a job. Don't focus on how difficult you think it is to get a job, focus on doing what you can to improve your chances and find a way to get a job.

At this present moment there may not be anything you can do to get a job. It may be late at night, you may be simply relaxing – if that's the case then simply focus on the present moment – be here now – reading this book. Don't focus on anything else –

just give all of your attention to reading this book and be here now.

When you look for work; focus on what has to be done at that moment. If your children need attention right now – then give them attention now. If you need to go out and look for work right now then go out and look for work right now.

Don't compare your present situation to anything, don't compare your present situation to what was, or what others have or what others are doing – accept what it is and make the most of it by doing what you can to make the present better with each step that you take. When you do this you improve your present situation and in the process you improve your future. Don't get me wrong – I'm not saying accept your present situation and don't do anything to improve it. I'm saying deal with your present situation and do everything you can to improve your life. The only way you can do that effectively is to be in the present moment – to be aware of everything that is going on and to do everything you can right now to improve your situation.

Once you begin working, living and being in the present moment with the intent of improving your life you begin to utilize the power of now – you leave the past in the past, you don't concentrate on the future and instead you start living in the present moment doing everything that you can to improve your life now. You no longer compare your life to what was or what might be – you simply focus on where you are now with the intent of improving your life and in the process – you will improve the lives of those around you.

When you do this you send a powerful message to your subconscious mind. You tell your subconscious that you are here now and that you are doing everything you can to improve your life now. Your subconscious mind then begins working for you because your subconscious only understands the present moment – your subconscious does not understand the future or the past – your subconscious only lives in the now – it is here now and in the present moment where it can be most effective.

While you may be able to understand and accept that being here now can give you tremendous power the challenge is in applying it. While many of you will be able to grasp and understand the concept of living in the now and working with the power of the present moment – practicing it is quite a different challenge. In order to practice living in the present and to utilize the Power Of Now you have to first start working with a process that involves getting your mind to work differently – something that your mind is not used to doing. But by working with this process you'll begin to live in the now while moving forward and improving your life because you'll be utilizing the power of now.

I once had a student named Josephine who had a terrible time letting go of the past. When she first called me about the Creating Power system she wanted to get a new job, she wanted to meet somebody and she wanted to start enjoying life. After a long conversation it was apparent that Josephine was still lamenting her financial loss from the stock market tumble of 2000, which was 3 years before I met her. Josephine had invested her life savings in technology stocks and lost everything – for the past 3 years she had been re-living the experience, thinking about how great her life was, how wonderful everything was until it all collapsed. When she got to that point she would move from the past to the future and focus on how miserable her life was going to be – she had decided that she could never make back the money she lost and the mere thought of going out into the world scared her to the point where she would just sit at home and do nothing.

Josephine started working with my Creating Power system and at times she felt overwhelmed because every time she thought of her goals or tried to get a plan together she would always look back to the loss she had endured, she would then decide she was a failure and that she was destined to be miserable. When we first started working together I would ask her what she would do for fun. She said nothing – "I can't think of anything." I had to take her back to the year 2000 and ask here what she did for fun back then. She finally explained that she liked to go to shopping malls, browse and spend some time at a bookstore. When I asked: "Now what do you like doing for fun." She would say: "Nothing." I realized I had to get her to begin living in the present moment – if Josephine was going to turn her life around she had to stop living in the year 2000, stop worrying about the future and start living in the present moment. We figured out her priorities – get a new job, meet someone, and get out of debt.

For 3 months we worked together along with my Creating Power system – everyday was a new challenge but after 3 months Josephine didn't think of what had happened in 2000 as much as she did when I first met her – a clear sign she was making progress. A few months later, Josephine had found a new job, she made a couple of new friends, she started going out to the malls and bookstores and she started to embrace life by appreciating what she had today, what she had right now and by focusing on what she could do at this present moment to improve her life. It was a one-day at a time process.

Josephine and I still keep in touch. She's in a relationship now, she hasn't made back the money she lost – but she has paid off a good chunk of her debt and she has a savings plan that she is sticking with. Everyday will be a new challenge for Josephine until she stops living in the past and focus on what is happening in her life right now. She will likely never forget the events of 2000 – but at least she no longer lets those events dominate her life and most importantly – she no longer lives in the year 2000 – for the most part – she's living in the present moment and her life is improving everyday.

The Present Is All That Exists

You may have memories of the past, you may have feelings when you think about the past, and you may worry about the future – but let's face it the past no longer exists. You can't step back in time and go into the past. Star Trek fans may disagree – but as far as we know – there is no way of going back in time and re-living or altering the past experiences. The past is done with. It doesn't exist. Similarly you can't step into the future and see what happens – despite what so called psychics and astrologers say – there is no way of seeing the future or living in the future. It hasn't happened – one day that future will arrive and if you're not paying attention – If you're too focused on the past or still worrying about the future – you'll miss it completely.

The only thing that is taking place right now is the present moment. As you read this chapter – that's all that you are doing. When you are done; the moment that you are currently experiencing will never happen again! The now will never happen again! Your present moment will never happen again!

Even when you think about the past – you do so in the present moment. You don't go back in time and remember the past – you do so in this present moment. When you think about the future you do it in the present moment – not in the future – you do it now. When you think about the past and the future you are wasting the valuable time and power that you have in the present moment. The only reason people are unhappy is because they fail to live in the present moment, they fail to embrace the now. Instead, they often think about what their present moment should be and allow their ego to dominate them – and when you do that the unhappiness sets in.

It is impossible to have a problem and live in the present moment at the same time. When you live in the present moment your attention is completely focused on what is happening right now. There are no thoughts of the future or the past. If you are at work – focus on work. If you are at home – focus on the home. If you are with friends – focus on your friends. When you do this your subconscious mind is released and free to start working on improving your life. When you are focused on the past or worried about the future – your subconscious is lost in confusion. It doesn't know what you want and is forced to go from present to past and present to future without being given the time or ability to create the situations you need to improve your life in the present moment. In short – you never allow your subconscious to function in the present moment – which is the only place that it can work. Your subconscious has its greatest power when you are living in the present moment.

Many of you may be seeking answers, trying to make decisions or just hoping to discover a passion that you can follow. All of these answers come when you live in the now – when you are focused on the present moment you will receive your answers. You can't step back into the past or step into the future to receive these answers, they only come in the present moment. But if you're focused on the past or consumed with the future then when the answer arrives you'll miss it. Why? Because you were not living in the present moment, which is the only place that you can receive the answer.

If you want to start directing your subconscious mind and if you want to stop living in the past and start living in the now then you need to take control of your mind and subconscious mind. Students who work with my Creating Power system learn how to let go of the past by getting their mind to work differently and they also start directing their subconscious mind to create the life they want. You can do the same and you can start by focusing on what is happening right now. Then begin to look at what you want to happen and look for ways to start doing what you can right now to achieve your goals. When you do this you force your mind to live in the present moment – which is where the subconscious mind is constantly working. The subconscious only knows what exists right now – when the mind is in the same place the two begin working together and you begin to get results sooner. You may not achieve your goal the very same day you start living in the present but you will make progress everyday when you are living in the now.

How To Live In The Now

The reason you and so many people have trouble living in the now is because your mind is simply not used to doing this. Your mind is used to remembering the past or worrying about the future – it can't live in the present because it doesn't know how. If you're right handed then compare the idea of getting the mind to work effectively, and with your subconscious mind similar to that of learning to do everything with your left hand. If you knew your life would improve dramatically if you simply used your left hand would it make things any easier? No it wouldn't. But if you practiced regularly and long enough after a while you would get used to using your left hand. Your mind is simply not used to living in the present moment – but as you train it – as you practice living in the now everyday your mind will get used to the process and your life would improve dramatically.

You can teach your mind how to live in the now and I'm about to outline some simple steps that you can take to start living in the now.

First take a look at your present situation and ask yourself what's wrong with the very moment you are in. Don't think about what happened yesterday or sometime in the past. Don't focus on what might or might not happen tomorrow. Take a look at the very moment you are in – I don't want you to think about another moment – just where you are now. Don't think about what will happen 5 minutes from now – focus only on what is happening now and see if there is anything wrong. If you are at home – is there something wrong?

Don't say you are out of work – that's not the present moment, it may be your overall situation, but it is not what is happening right now. Being out of work is what is not happening right now – focus on what is happening right now. I want you to focus your mind on what is happening at this very precise moment – then see what is wrong with that picture. My point is you should find nothing wrong with the present moment because the present is what it is. If you are home alone and the sun is shining outside then that is all that is happening. If you are home and it raining then it is simply raining and you are home. Focus on what is happening right now and once you start doing this you will be here now and you will begin living again – or you may begin living for the first time.

Let's face it you can't turn your mind off – but you can get your mind to work differently and that's what you should start doing. Because if you don't take control of your mind your mind will control you – and when that happens you will constantly be a slave to your mind and never be able to create changes or improvements in your life.

Ask yourself these next questions. Do you find yourself waiting for something to happen? Are you waiting to get some more time? Make more money? Meet the right person? Are you waiting for the right opportunity? Waiting is another game the mind plays because it doesn't want to live in the present moment. If you answered yes to any of the above questions then you are not living in the present moment – you are focusing on anything but the present moment because when you are here now there is no need to wait. If you want to make more money start working on a plan to make more money now. If you want to meet the right person – start doing something to meet the right person right now. If you are looking for the right opportunity then start looking for it now – don't wait for it to fall in your lap – do what you can in this present moment to begin improving your life.

I know you can't focus on the present moment or live in the now 24 hours a day. But start by doing this for a few minutes a day and then continue expanding the exercise everyday. For example: begin making it a habit to practice living in the now for a few minutes every morning. Do this for a full week and track your progress. See how you feel when you only focus on what is happening right now. As you continually do this you'll see yourself starting to enjoy the process. The following week – expand the exercise – make it a few minutes longer or do it twice during the day. The third week – expand again, or do the exercise three times a day – and continue doing this for a full year and see how you feel.

Here's a suggestion that will help you get started. The next time you are driving or walking pay attention only to what is happening around you. Listen to the sounds, observe the people. Don't think about what you have to do or what happened yesterday or what might happen tomorrow or what might happen in five minutes. Don't think about the problems of the day or what is wrong with your life. Focus your attention only on what is happening right now. Doing this will get your mind to start living in the present moment. As you continue doing this everyday, as you continue expanding the exercise everyday you'll soon be able to focus your mind and utilize the power of now. How will you know that you are truly utilizing the power of now? You'll begin finding solutions, you'll discover ways to improve your life, you'll be presented with new opportunities or you'll find these new opportunities yourself. In short – things will simply start falling into place and that would be a significant improvement.

Have Some Fun!

The final step in the process is to start having some fun. Start enjoying your life. Start doing things that you enjoy. Act like a 6 year old – don't try to be an adult all of the time. Forget about your troubles and just do something completely different – and have some fun. Once you start doing this you'll start enjoying life again, you'll see things begin to fall into place. If you have a passion for sports then start playing a sport you like. If you have a passion for cooking – make a meal or two over the next couple of days. Do what you enjoy and you'll start attracting more positive situations into your life.

The funny thing about the exercise I just described is that too many people have forgotten what it was like to simply enjoy life. Too many people have become adults and forgotten how to be a kid and enjoy life. Too many people are too busy being serious and forget how to have fun. Your spirit wants to enjoy life – it wants you to laugh and have fun. So do it – do what ever you want that will make you feel like a six year old again. Hang around some kids, behave like them and see how you feel. When you do this – you immediately begin enjoying life and living in the now – try it and see what happens.

My wife often teases me about being a big kid – sometimes she just can't take me seriously. But the best part is that we laugh a lot. She's sometimes a bigger kid than I am – and that's not easy to do but it allows us both to have a lot of fun and in the process of laughing and enjoying life – you simply cannot be upset, angry or sad. Try it – see if you can laugh and be angry? See if you can laugh and be sad? It's simply not possible.

I remember working with a student who had a ton of goals and laundry list of things that needed to change. Most of them I thought were not all that bad – but she thought that her whole life was a mess. I asked her to think back to when she was 6 or 7 years old and playing with her friends on the weekend. I asked her what she did – and she explained they used to have water gun fights. They would raid her brother's room, gather his water pistols, fill them up and have a water gun fight. I suggested she go out and buy a water gun. She had 2 children, aged 7 and 10. I asked her to get them water guns and then have a good old-fashioned water gun fight. She thought I was crazy. (By the way I used to be big on water gun fights and would often target people in my newsroom when I was working as a reporter in New York – it was my way of acting like a kid and breaking the tension). I egged her on and finally she bought the water guns. It took her a few more weeks to engage her children in a little mischief – but after she did she said she hadn't felt so good in years. The water gun fights became a regular thing in her household and after a while she started doing more stuff with her kids.

During the process this student got closer to her children, began to feel more relaxed and said that usually after an hour or even less of acting like a kid she would often come up with solutions to some of the challenges she faced or experienced tremendous bursts of creative energy.

Now some of the most successful people in the world engage in their own childish acts or they find another way to blow off some steam and have some fun. Larry Ellison, CEO of Oracle Corp. and one of the richest men in the world sails often, it's something he enjoys and takes seriously – but it's not work. Richard Branson, also one of the richest men in the world, enjoys extreme sports. Some of them like to play golf, hunt, fish, or skydive – like former U.S. President George Bush. My point is that they all find time to enjoy life. Today I no longer have water gun fights – sure I act like a kid at home – but I also play soccer 2 or 3 times a week – just because it's something that I've always enjoyed doing. You also have a passion – something that you enjoy doing – but are you doing it? If not – now is the time to start.

I had a friend, André, who loved playing basketball – not organized basketball – just a game of pickup every weekend. But after he got married and had a child he found he was no longer playing basketball. He said life was just too hectic. As our conversation continued André explained that he just didn't seem to be having any more fun, life just seemed to be too routine and it seemed like he was existing but not living, sure things were hectic – but he just wasn't having any fun.

I suggested he start playing basketball again – in fact – I urged him to start playing again and asked him to call some old friends and get a game going. At the time he was fed up with his job – no longer satisfied with it and was yearning for a change. He didn't know what he wanted – he knew he just needed a change.

André started playing basketball – at first it was just a few guys but after a few weeks they had enough for two 5 a side teams. One of the guys had just moved to the city and was looking to start up a small furniture business. André loved buying old furniture – he told me he would often walk around the city looking for antiques that had been overlooked or go antiquing with his wife on weekends. He didn't want antiques – he just liked the old style of furniture. The two players got to know each other and after playing for over a year they started a small business – a furniture shop that specializes in replicating old style furniture – antique style furniture without the antique furniture prices.

By having some fun and just focusing on being in the present moment André found his passion – while following another passion – playing pick-up basketball. When you follow your passion, when you do what you enjoy, when you live in the present moment – you get back on track and end up doing what you really want. It all flows naturally – because you're opening yourself up to greater possibilities and you're doing things just for the fun of it, while being here now – you're no longer letting your ego dominate. You're just having fun. You're no longer worrying about what will happen tomorrow, or what happened yesterday – you're just enjoying the present moment by doing what you enjoy doing.

I've given you some exercises and shown you how to start living in the present moment and how to utilize the Power Of Now – the rest is up to you. It's your choice – you can live in the present, start working with the exercises, start being in the present and you'll start seeing some dramatic improvements in your life.

Here now are some questions from students and newsletter subscribers about living in the present moment and utilizing the Power Of Now.

Question:
"I lost my job a few years ago and I haven't been able to find steady work since the stock market crash of 2000. I know I have to move on but I just can't seem to stop thinking about what happened and how much I suffered. When I think about it I am taken over by fear. What should I do?"
-Stanislov, Croatia

Answer:
Hi Stanislov,
The first thing in moving forward is to now begin focusing on what you want now. The past happened, learn from it and begin moving forward by focusing on what you want now. The only reason you continually think about the past and

what happened is because that's what your mind knows and that's what your mind is used to. So to get your mind moving in a new direction you have to give it something new to focus on – and that is what you want to have happen in your life now. Next – when you find that you are thinking about the past – stop. Start focusing on what is going on in your life at that precise moment. If you are walking down a street and you start thinking about the past, stop and focus on what is happening around you, simply observe and be in that present moment by thinking of and experiencing exactly what is happening right now. Things won't change overnight but the sooner you start working with the exercises I've just outlined the sooner you'll start moving forward. Finally – you'll have to do these exercises on a regular basis – everyday, throughout the day at different intervals of the day. The more often you do this the sooner you'll release the past and start creating a new life.

Question:

"I moved to the United States several years ago and while I enjoy this country I can't stop thinking of my home, my family and the life I used to have. When I do I get very sad – I want to move forward but I can't seem to let go of the past and the life that I once had. Here I have no one – there I have everything. What can I do?"
-Jason, T.

Answer:

Hi Jason,

Thanks for writing. You should first start thinking about what you really want. While you are in the U.S. it seems that you long to be with your family but at the same time enjoy being in the U.S. Think about what you want and remember – you don't have to give up one or the other. You certainly can enjoy living in the U.S. and then take time to be with your family by either visiting them or having them come visit you. Open yourself up to new possibilities and you will find solutions. Enjoy the place that you are in – make the most of the time that you are in the U.S. – when you are with your family make the most of the time that you have with them. Things can change at anytime and when you enjoy the moment that you are in – you'll actually be able to discover new possibilities to make what you want a reality. When you think of your family and the life you had – appreciate your family and then begin enjoying the place that you are in. Enjoy what is happening right now, and when you have a chance think of what you want and how you can make what you want happen. Remember – anything is possible.

Question:

"I broke up with my boyfriend 2 years ago. I have tried to get back with him but he wants nothing to do with me. At first after we broke up we stayed good friends but now he won't even speak to me.

He has a new girlfriend and I just can't seem to let go. In my heart I know we are right for each other – but he won't come back. Any advice would be helpful."
-Indira.

Answer:
Hi Indira,
If your boyfriend wants nothing to do with you why would you want to be with him? Why would you want to be with someone who doesn't even want to speak with you? If he truly was the right person then things would work out nice and easily – but at this point you are not even giving yourself the chance to meet someone. If you truly want to move on and begin enjoying life then look at where you are now and what kind of life you want. Start living in the now by realizing that you are here now and that your ex-boyfriend is not. This is your life and you can now live the life you want. You can choose to be in the past – which doesn't exist – or you can start living in the present moment and begin attracting and being with the right person – the person who will be with you for a very long time. When you think of your ex-boyfriend – tell yourself: "He's not here – I am and now I am creating my new life and I am attracting the right person – the man who is everything I want and more." Then begin experiencing the present moment that you are in. If you are with friends, be with them; enjoy their company, experience the

moment – a moment that will never come again. Think about what you want and start doing what you can to make that happen. Your future awaits, your present moment is here now – you can only begin to experience the wonders of life when you release the past, live in the now and embrace your future.

Question:

"I used to be a star athlete and almost became a professional football player. That was years ago – but I just can't seem to get those glory days out of my head. I try everything – but I just can't seem to enjoy life. I know I can't play football anymore – but I really want to enjoy life."
-Help

Answer:

The star athlete that you once were no longer exists. But it seems that you want the recognition and importance of being a star athlete and being involved in football. It's interesting that you know that you can't play football anymore – so what else can you do that will give you the same significance. Could you coach? Could you work with younger aspiring football players? If you're not involved with the game on any level – I would suggest you get involved. I would also recommend that you start looking at all of the positive things that are taking place in your life now. By focusing on the present moment and living in the now – you'll begin to appreciate what is going on in your life right now. Yes you can enjoy those glory days – only they will be different. You may not be a star athlete – but you can certainly begin being a star human being.

creatingpower.com

7

Power Of Patience

"When written in Chinese, the word "crisis"
is composed of two characters. One represents
danger and the other represents opportunity."
- John F. Kennedy

Throughout this book I've been giving you different tips, different exercises, different techniques that will help you achieve your goals. Let's face it we all want results. We all want changes, we all could do with some improvements in our lives. Even the most successful and happiest people in the world will tell you that there is always room for improvement. With the pace of life today, with the advances in computers, cell phones and fast foods – most of us now want things instantly. When I worked in the news business if someone would ask how soon you wanted something done, the answer was: "I want it yesterday." It seems today we all want things done yesterday.

When you're dealing with technology it certainly is possible to have things immediately and instantly. But we are human beings – we are not a piece of technology. We are thinking, growing, and evolving creatures capable of accomplishing tremendous feats. We are part of nature – 70-percent of our bodies are water – 70-percent of the earth's surface is water. When we die, the parts of our bodies that aren't liquefied turn to dust. In the end we return to nature – unlike technology we are a part of nature. And unlike anything created by human beings – we work best when we are in sync' with nature and when we understand that we are on nature's clock. Not ours and not technology's clock – but nature's clock.

When you begin to understand this you begin to utilize another power that you have – and this is the power of patience.

I'm not asking you to sit around and wait for things to magically change – nothing could be further from the truth. Instead, the power of patience requires that you understand and accept that when you start focusing on making major changes in your life, when you start working with all of the other techniques and exercises I outlined – the changes you seek will happen. But they will happen when you are patient, when you trust and believe that the changes and improvements you want will in fact happen.

Remember – there is a process at work and part of this process requires that you be patient and trust that everything is already working out.

Are you among the millions of people who would like to see things happen in an instant? Do you find that you want to get something done, achieve a goal but would like it to happen now? Well if you are – then you may actually be doing yourself more harm than good. That's because in order to excel in life and achieve your goals you need to utilize the power of patience and when you are impatient, when you demand that things change instantly only to get frustrated or angry when they don't – then you are working against the Power of Patience and in the process you may be doing yourself more harm than good.

In the years of teaching my Creating Power system I've noticed that more and more it seems people are becoming impatient and what is strikingly interesting is that the more impatient they are the further away they are from achieving their goals. If we had our way we would have things yesterday, when we decide we want to achieve something we want to achieve that goal right away, and when we decide we want to change or that we want to improve ourselves we also want those things to happen right away. But if we look at human beings as part of nature – which is exactly what we are – and if we examine nature carefully you suddenly realize that nature doesn't create change in an instant.

Ralph Waldo Emerson perhaps said it best in one simple line:

"Adopt the pace of nature, her secret is patience" –

and having that patience can lead to the perfect life – if you understand how to work with the power of patience and nature together.

Why Patience Is Critical to Success

Ask any successful businessman or entrepreneur and they'll tell you that they never rush into a decision. Sure they'll follow their gut instinct – but they'll take plenty of time researching, studying and thinking – waiting until the right moment to make a decision.

When you examine nature's process you find that it works in a similar fashion and has a great deal of patience – in nature things develop over a period of time and everything comes together only at the right time. For example: you plant a seed, water it, leave it for some time, then at the right time – when all the right elements are in place – that seed begins to sprout its roots, starts to grow and turns into a flower, a vegetable or whatever it is that you planted. But this only happens when the conditions are right. However, there was work to be done before those elements came into place. The seed had to be planted, it had to be nurtured, it had to be left alone to begin to grow and spring roots under the soil, then at the right time – it began to rise above the surface into exactly what it was meant to be.

Without the prior efforts, without the planting, the watering and the incubation period – the seed could not have sprung above the ground. It would not have been what it is today without all that work.

If you want to achieve your goals – you have to practice patience. That doesn't mean you sit around and wait. No, instead you have to do the work first, lay the foundation, plant the seed, make sure the soil is right – prepare and then wait for all the right elements to come into place before making the right decision that will propel you to greater success.

Unfortunately most people don't practice this process and by not working with this process they end up feeling pressed to change things instantly. This happens only because they feel a sense of urgency – things have become so bad that they must change right away. While the change will happen – it rarely will happen at your pace or right away. And if you're not willing to accept that then maybe you can take comfort in knowing that if you don't practice the power of patience – all the things you seek to change and accomplish will likely never happen or you will likely never feel fulfilled. The choice is yours – learn to practice the power of patience or live life with an empty feeling. I know what choice I would make.

When you refuse to practice some degree of patience you ignore the process of nature; you then end up reacting to situations or you look for the next quick solution. By adopting this "quick fix" approach you work against nature and in the end get pushed back further.

If you want to be successful and achieve your goals you have to practice a certain amount of patience – and this type of patience is something I teach to each of my students who work with my Creating Power system. I said I don't want you to sit around and wait – so let me explain exactly what kind of patience I am talking about.

You have gone through most of this book to arrive at this point. You have selected your goals and hopefully you've started utilizing the various techniques I've outlined and begun working with the different powers that I have discussed. Now you must listen, watch, observe, pay attention to things, examine and see what opportunities are right for you. You must trust that you have done your work and you have planted your seeds, which will now start to grow. You must think of what else you can do and then do what needs to be done as often as you can. If you have done all that you feel you can do for the day – move on with the other things that you can do in other areas of your life.

For example: If you are looking for a new job and you have worked with all of the exercises that I have outlined, and now you have taken the right action – you have sent out your resumes, you have talked to friends, gone on the interview for the day – now rest and trust that you will get the right job. Don't sit anxiously by the phone. Don't pace up and down throughout your home. Relax, be patient and go about doing what you have to do. Tomorrow – go through the process of looking and getting a job again and see what you come up with – always being patient and always trusting that you are being guided to the right job or that you will find the right way to make more money.

Patience is something you get better at with practice – but if you have little or no patience – your impatience will work against you.

How Impatience Works Against You

When you're impatient – when you don't trust and accept that things will work out – you actually get slowed down, distracted or end up on the wrong track – then you may wonder: "How did I get here?" It's a process that ends up putting you further away from your goals and actually works against you.

Here's an example: suppose you're in line waiting to pay for something – and it's a rather long line and there's another cashier with an equally long line. If you huff and get angry – it won't change anything. If you jump to the other line – it may actually take longer (I'm sure many of you have had this happen), if you leave – you quit and don't get what you want. Sometimes you'll leave saying you'll come back when the line is shorter – but you don't know when that will be and there's a good chance that you'll never go back in which case you still didn't get what you wanted. So by being impatient you either got angry, thought the grass was greener on the other side and went to the other line where you may have ended up waiting longer or you quit and never got what you wanted. Had you been patient, chances are you would have made your payment and moved on. I know some of you will say: "Yeah but what happens when the other line does move faster – I'm not going to stay where I am." Of course you won't – but when that happens you can switch lines – remember – you're waiting for the right moment. My point is that you shouldn't assume that the grass is greener on the other side – deal with the situations you are presented with, focus on making the right decisions, be patient knowing that you are going to make the right decision and you'll make the right decision.

Now let's take a look at something that is a little more serious – and this is something I hear a lot about. Let's say you want to increase your finances and you want to make a million dollars – I have a lot of people call me and tell me that they want to make a million dollars right away. I then tell them that while anything is possible – making a million dollars right away is unlikely to happen. Some get angry and hang up because I didn't tell them what they wanted to hear and they didn't get the quick fix that they were looking for. But here's why it's unlikely to happen right away or even in 3 months: there is a process that needs to take place. Just like that seed can't grow above the ground in 3-days; just like that seed has to go through its natural process, so do you – and part of that process is growing, adjusting to the point where your mind becomes comfortable with the possibility that you can make a million dollars – to the point where you believe you can make a million dollars, learning the right formula that will help you make a million dollars and then begin the process of making a million dollars. Sure you could look for that quick fix, make risky investments, try different schemes, gamble, buy lottery tickets – but you would likely lose more money by working with that process – a process which in most cases goes against the laws of nature.

When you work with the power of patience and understand that you are working in synchronicity with nature – you would then start laying a foundation to make a million dollars. This could mean doing something like starting a business and increasing your revenue year over year. You could start with more solid investments – and build on them year over year. You could come up with a solid financial plan and build on it year over year. The notion of getting things right away ignores the process of nature, eliminates the power of patience and will just set you back further.

Unfortunately in today's society we want instant satisfaction. We want something that will fix everything right away. We want a pill that will cure everything. We want our food ready in an instant. But nature doesn't work instantly and we are creatures of nature – we are part of nature. We operate on the same schedule and the same platform. We start off as infants, grow to adults, age and pass on. Just like aspects of nature.

Success in life doesn't happen overnight. Creating a business and making it a success requires patience. Establishing a career and moving up in a company takes time and requires patience. Making investments that payoff in the long-term take time and requires patience. Planting a seed that will grow into a wonderful plant takes time and requires patience. Having impatience in business or in life is like inviting disaster. Relationships take time to build and improve – having impatience in a relationship is a sure way to end it. Finding the right job requires patience and effort, having impatience in a job search is a sure way to get rejected.

In all of the above examples and other aspects of life things can happen in an instant – but your success in them will require time, effort and patience. For example: You may meet a partner tomorrow – but the success of that relationship will require patience – so that the relationship has the time to grow and succeed. You could come up with a business idea tomorrow – but its success will require time, effort and patience. You could find a job tomorrow – but your success at it will depend on how much time and effort you put in and how patient you are not only on the job but also with co-workers and bosses.

If you want balance and harmony, if you want success and happiness you have to do all that you can and then utilize the power of patience.

How Patience Pays Off

I can best illustrate how the power of patience

brings enormous rewards with an example of Peter – and old friend of mine who has had a very successful career and rewarding life.

10 years ago Peter and another friend Desmond, started working at the same company – both had similar entry-level positions and both had great ambitions. Peter was always the more patient laid back type – whereas Desmond was on the hyper side - always itching to get something done, showing little patience and always wanting to move up in the company quickly. After a year on the job Desmond was already looking to move on and find something new. He demanded a higher salary or a promotion – threatening to leave. A few months later he left the company and tried to talk Peter into doing the same thing. Peter – chose to stay. Desmond went from job to job – always looking for something better. The longest he's ever stayed at a job has been 2 years. When I last spoke to him Desmond was out of work and looking again. He said his name had been tarnished because he had gone through so many companies in such a short period of time. "I guess they just don't want somebody who has no patience with management." He explained when we had lunch. I thought it was fascinating – his impatience had actually worked against him.

Peter is still with that same company and is now a Senior Manager in line to be Vice President of his own division within a few years. His salary has tripled and he has the seniority and respect of his superiors. "I guess they just like the fact that I've stayed and put up with them. It has its up and downs – but I try to focus on the good and hope my patience will pay off." I recall Peter saying when I spoke to him just before writing this chapter.

The power of patience is truly incredible – you have no idea how many good things can happen to those who practice patience. I'm not asking you to sit around and wait for things to happen – I never ask any of my students to do that and I am a firm believer in taking action. But I am also a firm believer in understanding that when you set a goal you have to practice patience – then only will you see the true payoff. Desmond didn't practice patience and it worked against him. Peter did practice patience and it paid off in numerous ways. The Power of Patience requires an understanding that things take time to happen – that you do the work and you reap the benefits when the time is right.

If you planted a seed and stood over it waiting for it to sprout through the ground, you'd go crazy. If you planted a seed and ignored it – it would die. If you planted a seed and placed a rock on top of it – it would never flourish. But if you planted a seed and did the work to help it grow, and cared for it –

that seed would turn into a plant that would flourish and thrive.

The same applies in life. Do your work, do the best that you can – be patient and understand that things will fall into place at the right time. If you want a new job – do what you can to find a new job, go out and do the work, but then practice patience – knowing that it will come at the right time. I know some of you may say: "Karim, I need the job now." Remember – your impatience will work against you. But if you utilize the powers of your mind and subconscious mind as I outline in my Creating Power system and as I've outlined in throughout this book you'll be able to attract the right job and the right situation at the right time.

What ever it is you want to happen in your life – it will arrive in time as long as you work with the power of your mind and subconscious mind. Some of you may say: "Karim, I've been patient a long time but nothing has happened. I'm sick of waiting – I can't wait any longer." I'm not asking you to wait. But for those who may say something like that I have the following questions: Have you done everything you can to improve the situation? Have you worked with the powers of your mind and subconscious mind on a regular basis so that you attract the right situation? If not then ask yourself why not? Why aren't you giving yourself every opportunity to succeed in life? Why aren't you developing the power of your mind and subconscious mind? Is wishful thinking getting you any closer to what you want to achieve?

Patience is not about waiting – it's about doing everything you can and understanding that everything will fall into place at the right time and then being aware of when that time arrives so that you can capitalize on the opportunity to improve your life dramatically.

Practicing Patience

Now I know that for those of you who are not patient – or who have not practiced patience very often in your life this process may seem a little challenging for you. So I'm going to outline how you can begin practicing patience in simple ways through out the day. By doing this you'll get more comfortable with the process, begin to develop confidence in the Power of Patience until you are able to fully integrate and practice patience in every area of your life so that you see magnificent results and achieve your goals.

As you go through your day think about the little things that you want to accomplish. For example: if you want to get to work on time then focus on getting to work on time. Tell yourself that you are getting to work on time. Then be patient – go about your normal routine, take the normal route to work and if you feel like making any changes in your plan – focus on making the right decision and see what you decide then see what happens, see if you get to work on time. It may not work out the first day – but as you do this more often you'll see that you'll be getting to work on time more often than not. If you're at work and you're dealing with people – be a little more patient with them – and again focus on what you want to happen – then exercise some patience – see if things start to get better. If you are in a relationship – exercise a little more patience with your partner – think about what you want to happen, focus on it and be patient. Exercise patience whenever you can throughout the day and then see what kind of outcome you get, but remember; focus on what you want. I'm not asking that you allow yourself to be pushed around or that you be forced to wait. Instead, focus on what you want to happen, do things to make that happen and then work with the power of patience and see what kind of results you get. The more often you do this the better you'll get at it and the better your results will be.

During the time that you are patient – be observant – don't just ignore everything that takes place. Pay attention to what is happening because during this time of patience you will either get ideas that will help you accomplish what you want, you could get suggestions from friends or colleagues that will help you accomplish your goals, you may get some information from a completely unexpected source – but you will be guided during this incubation period and when you start seeing these things happen it's important that you follow up on them and investigate – see what works for you.

I know that many of you want to see improvements or changes right away. Some of you will also want to accomplish your goals right away – you may want to be a millionaire overnight – but remember what I said – there is a process at work and you have to learn to work with that process in order to achieve your goals. The process of change can begin right away – it can start today – if you simply begin working with the techniques and exercises that I have outlined in this book. The dramatic changes that you want to see will also happen over time – and when they do they will be long lasting changes that will allow you to enjoy life and experience true happiness – all you have to do is exercise a little patience.

As in every chapter I've included some questions that have been emailed to me on the subject of patience. These are from students working with my Creating Power system and subscribers to my weekly email newsletter. I think you'll find some of them quite insightful.

Question:
"I am sick and tired of waiting. I have been waiting

for something good to come my whole life and I have had no luck. You talk of patience, I have had plenty of patience and I'm still waiting. I guess I'll just wait for the next life – unless you have a better suggestion?"
-Boston, MA

Answer:

Waiting is exactly what you should not be doing. You say you've been patient but I think you equate patience with waiting – they are two entirely different things. When you are patient you are constantly working towards your goals and doing everything that you can to improve your life while being aware that the right opportunity could present itself at anytime. When you are waiting you are merely wasting time – waiting for something good to happen as you put it will never yield results. The only way something good can happen is when you actually begin taking steps toward making the good that you seek happen in your life. So I suggest you decide what it is you want to happen – that is; decide what good you want in your life, then start working with a plan, train your mind to focus on achieving your goal, direct your subconscious mind to create opportunities for you to achieve your goals and begin doing something everyday to create the life you want. Once you get started you'll immediately recognize the difference between waiting and being patient.

Question:

"If I want to achieve a particular goal why should I have to be patient? Should I not be able to instruct my subconscious mind to create what I want right away? Why should I have to do any work? Why can't my subconscious mind just bring it to me? Please explain."
-Doug H., New York.

Answer

Spoken like a true New Yorker. Doug if you're thirsty would you sit on your couch and wait for a glass of water to magically appear before your eyes? Or would you get up and get it? The latter would require work and it is likely what most of us would do. So if you want to achieve your goal then you should start doing everything you can to make it a reality. In the process your subconscious mind will guide you to the right opportunity. In some cases you can achieve your goals immediately – if all the elements are in place and you are able to recognize the right opportunity when it is presented you may very well be able to achieve your goal right away. But sometimes it takes a little longer for all the elements to come into place in order for you to achieve your goal. You may or may not have developed the ability to recognize the right opportunity at the right time. If you have not developed the ability to recognize the right opportunity, or if you have not yet discovered the right opportunity then it may take a little longer. If you're in great shape then you may be able to run a marathon your first time out. If you're not – then you may not complete it the first time out. The same process applies in life – how quickly you achieve your goals, how quickly you instruct your subconscious mind and how quickly you eliminate the negative thinking so that you can achieve your goals depends on what kind of shape your mind is in. I am simply teaching you how to train your mind and subconscious mind so that they are in optimum shape – then you'll be able to achieve your goals.

Question:

"I have been in a relationship with the same man for 6 years but he won't make the ultimate commitment. When we speak of marriage he changes the subject. I have been patient but I am tired of waiting. What can I do to resolve this situation?"
-Tanya S., Oregon

Answer:

Hi Tanya,
You first have to decide if you want to get married or if you're happy where you are. Assume your boyfriend never wants to get married – now what? Would you want to stay or leave? There's no law that says that you have to get married. Now, let's focus on what you want. If you really do want to get married and you want to marry the person you

are with – which I think is the case, then start finding ways to talk to him about getting married. Your goal is to get married to him but your goal should also be to understand why he is afraid of marriage, and help him understand that marriage can be a wonderful thing. Don't try to control him. Don't try to force your opinion and viewpoint on him. Start focusing on finding a solution, on finding a way to help your boyfriend understand the benefits of marriage, on finding a way to communicate with him about marriage without scaring him off and you'll find answers. There is a certain amount of patience that you will have to exercise because it could take some time to find the right approach – but if what you are doing isn't working – then try a different approach. Focus on the solution, be open-minded and be willing to work with him and you will.

Question:
"Karim, my mind seems to be all over the place. When I set a goal I get very anxious, I get nervous and I want to achieve that goal right away. Then my mind wonders off to another goal and I end up getting very negative and depressed because I never get anything done. I never achieve any goal that I set out to achieve. I am 36 years old now and I really need to gain control of my mind. How can you help?"
-Thomas T, Australia.

Answer:

Hi Thomas,

The first thing you should do is to track your mind to get a better idea of exactly how it works. Keep track of your thoughts, write down the thoughts that you feel are scattered or unfocused. Set a simple goal and get your mind to focus on that goal throughout the day. When you catch your mind drifting – bring it back by focusing on that one simple goal. It can be anything – like getting to work on time, or meeting a friend at a particular time. See how your mind performs on the simple goals. Then as you get more comfortable with this process aim for bigger goals and begin instructing your subconscious mind to work toward these goals with the exercises I've outlined in my Creating Power system. These will help you a great deal. As for the anxiety – this is usually triggered by a thought or a series of thoughts. The next time you experience the anxiety stop and try to recall the thought you had that triggered that anxiety. See if the thoughts are realistic, and then start changing your thoughts to focus on what you want. This is the first step in training your mind and re-directing your subconscious mind but as you work with all of the exercises I've outlined you'll begin to see changes taking place.

8

Staying Motivated

"Winners are those people who make a habit of doing the things losers are uncomfortable doing."
- Ed Foreman

Now that you know what you have to do, now that you are working with the techniques that I've outlined, and now that you are developing and implementing the Power Of Believing – you have to stay motivated. For some – staying motivated can be the biggest challenge. It's not enough to know what to do – your power comes from your ability to do what you know, do it regularly and do it well. Let's face it – we all know that we should eat better, eat healthy foods, avoid fats and fried foods – but how many of us actually do it? If we all did we'd all be healthier and likely live longer, more productive lives. We all know how to run – but how many of us actually go jogging every morning or run in a marathon? If we all did we'd probably be a lot healthier and in much better physical shape. You now know how to develop and utilize the Power of Believing – those of you that practice all of the exercises will enjoy happier, successful and more rewarding lives. Those of you who give up, quit, or say: "I know this stuff" and not do anything, or those of you who say: "I know this stuff – it's not for me" will likely not make any progress and see little improvements in your life. The key to your success is to now do what you know and stay motivated.

So how do you stay motivated? Simple. You stay motivated by focusing on the end result of what you want. You stay motivated by keeping in mind the rewards that come with achieving your goal, changing aspects of your life and making significant improvements. This process requires that you keep in mind the motivating factor – which in many cases is very different from the goal you want to achieve.

For example: you may want to make millions of dollars or you may want to make a lot of money – but having the money is not necessarily the motivating factor. That is; the money itself won't change your life. It's what that money will do for you that will change your life. If you wanted more money so that you could stop working so hard – then the motivating factor is the freedom of being able to do what you want when you want. If you wanted to make more money so that you could buy a new home – then your motivating factor is living comfortably in a spacious new home in a better, safer neighborhood. If you wanted to make more money so that you could send your children to college, university or a private school – then your motivating factor would be to give your children a better education and a better chance at living a successful life. The money itself isn't the motivating factor – it's what the money can do for you or what you can do with the money that really motivates you.

Understanding your motivating factor is important because this is what drives you. So what I want you to do now is to list your goals again and this time beside each goal write down the motivating factor. Be honest – only you will see this information. I've given you room for 10 goals – you may have more – stick to the ten most important goals right now – but as you list them again you may find that some goals overlap – that's okay – you can always combine goals. If you have less than 10 goals – that's okay, you don't have to have 10 goals – focus on what is most important right now – focus on the changes that will improve the quality of your life and list the motivating factor. You may have to think a little bit before deciding the motivating factor – that's okay you can always come back and change or fine tune your motivating factor. I suggest you use the space that I've provided to complete this exercise.

Goals and Motivating Factors

Goal 1	Motivating Factor
Goal 2	Motivating Factor
Goal 3	Motivating Factor
Goal 4	Motivating Factor
Goal 5	Motivating Factor
Goal 6	Motivating Factor
Goal 7	Motivating Factor
Goal 8	Motivating Factor
Goal 9	Motivating Factor
Goal 10	Motivating Factor

Now that you know your motivating factor for each of your goals you know what to focus on. When you think of achieving those goals, when you think of taking steps to make those goals a reality – think of the motivating factor – because that's what drives you. Here's an example:

Two people – Janet and Debra want to lose weight, and get in shape. They both agree to go on a diet and exercise – so they also join a gym. At night they both agree to plan their meals for the next day so that they eat better. They both also agree to set their alarms for 7 in the morning so they can get to the gym and workout before getting to work.

Every night Janet prepares her breakfast, lunch and plans her meal for dinner. In the morning, Janet leaps out of bed when her alarm clock goes off, gets ready, has her well-prepared breakfast and goes to the gym. She does a solid workout for 90-minutes before going to work. Janet sticks to her diet and continues her workouts for a full 90-days. She's not crazy about getting up in the morning, she doesn't like cutting out all the sweets and fatty foods that taste so good, and she's really not crazy about exercising. But she knows that if she wants to look great and be in terrific shape – this is what she has to do so she sticks with it.

Debra rarely plans her meals before going to bed. When the alarm clock goes off she hits the snooze button and before she knows it – she has to get to work – no time for a workout. Breakfast is usually a buttered muffin with a coffee – lunch is whatever she craves and she almost always dines out – never sticking to her diet.

After 90-days – who do you think lost more weight?

Janet loses the weight and is able to do the things she does because she's focused on the result – to her the reward of being slim, fit and looking great is the prize that she is after. And she knows that if she sticks to her routine she'll lose the weight, get in shape and look great. She doesn't think about the process, she doesn't think about having to wake up early, and not eating what she wants. She stays focused on the reward, which is to get in shape, lose weight and look great.

Debra is only focused on the immediate reward – which is to eat what she wants and do what she wants. She's not concerned about the long-term reward and after 90-days instead of losing weight she put on more weight. Debra also focuses on the process – she dreads the thought of getting up early, changing her eating habits and going for a workout. She's not concerned about the long-term goal. Now the prize of being fit and looking great is even further out of reach because she didn't focus on the motivating factor – which was to be slim, in shape and look great. Instead she's worse off than when she started and now she wants the results immediately so she'll try the latest fad diet and any pill that promises to help her lose weight – but it will never happen because she's not focusing on the right objective.

Unfortunately most of the world consists of people like Debra – they're not focusing on the motivating factor – which is the long-term result that you're after. Results don't happen overnight – but you can make progress overnight. You can begin to lose weight one day at a time. You can begin to make more money one day at a time; you can begin to move closer to achieving your goals one day at a time if you focus on your motivating factor.

Now that you have your motivating factor – don't be like Debra – be like Janet and keep the motivating factor in mind. Remember why the goal is important and think of what you can do everyday to continue moving toward that goal.

Debra focused on the process and as a result didn't like the fact that she had to prepare her meals at night, change her eating habits at breakfast, lunch and dinner and didn't like the fact that she had to get up in the morning and go to the gym. This is the process that helps her achieve her goals and when she thought of the process – the little, painful things that have to be done – she thought quitting was a better option but in the end it only set her back further. By focusing on the process Debra came up with a laundry list of excuses for not sticking to her commitment – there was always an excuse for not getting things done. You may find that you do this at times – you may find that you come up with an explanation to justify why you did not get something done. The only person you're cheating in this case is yourself. Now there are legitimate reasons – and I don't dismiss these – but how many are truly legitimate reasons and how many are just lame excuses that give you a way out of doing something you know will help you accomplish your goals and improve your life – if you focused on the end result.

So why do people do this? Why do we come up with excuses and create what we think is a valid explanation for not getting things done? Because that's what you're used to doing, it's because that's what you and your mind are used to doing. Let's face it we're all creatures of habit and once we get used to doing something we just stick with it. Think about it. You have a routine that you likely follow every morning, and you just follow certain habits throughout the day that you've developed. Unfortunately when it comes to achieving your goals many have developed the habit of making excuses and finding reasons not to get things done. Now if only you could put aside the excuses and get motivated you would be able to move forward and start achieving your goals.

Think about it – is there something that you've

been meaning to do but just haven't been able to for the longest time? I'm not talking about a specific goal—just something that you've been meaning to do but haven't been able to.

What's the reason? Think about it. Why have you been putting it off for so long? Write it down and you'll discover your excuses—these are the reasons why you're not getting motivated. To make it easier I've provided some space below for you to do this. This exercise is only for you and it will help you identify the legitimate reasons and the poor excuses for not getting things done. Once you've got a handle on this you'll discover the areas where you need to focus on the motivating factor instead of the process. The process is tedious, it's painful, it's no fun – but it has to be done because by going through the process you're able to achieve your goals.

Professional Basketball players sometimes practice twice a day and these guys are professionals – yet they still go through that tedious process of going to the court and practicing. I'm sure many of them would much rather be doing something else but they understand that the process is necessary in order to achieve their goal of winning.

Now it's important to understand just what is getting in your way so that you can change it and overcome this issue and then motivate yourself to success and happiness. So use the space below to write down the reasons why you haven't been able to do something that you have been meaning to do for some time.

What I wanted To Do	Reason For Not Doing It
What I wanted To Do	Reason For Not Doing It
What I wanted To Do	Reason For Not Doing It
What I wanted To Do	Reason For Not Doing It
What I wanted To Do	Reason For Not Doing It

What I wanted To Do	Reason For Not Doing It
What I wanted To Do	Reason For Not Doing It

You may not be able to fill up all of the space and that's okay – do what you can. If you need more space – stick with what you've written down and we'll go from there.

Once you've done this exercise you can go back to your list and highlight those that are just excuses while circling those that are legitimate reasons. You have to decide what is a legitimate reason – I usually think something like: being out of work, not having any money as possible legitimate reasons – but you can find work and you can make some money. So what is a legitimate reason? That's for you to decide – all I ask is that you be fair and be honest with yourself.

Now that you know where you are making excuses let's take a look at those things that you wanted to do but didn't. In the following space you're going to list those things that you wanted to do but made up excuses for not doing them – but now you're going to think about the motivating factor, and beside what you wanted to do – list the motivating factor (why you wanted to do that).

What I wanted to do	Motivating Factor
What I wanted to do	Motivating Factor
What I wanted to do	Motivating Factor
What I wanted to do	Motivating Factor
What I wanted to do	Motivating Factor

Now you know the motivating factor for what you wanted to do but instead came up with excuses. The next time you decide to do something on the list – think about the motivating factor – because that's the result you really want – that's what ultimately drives you.

Here are some of the excuses and reasons that I hear everyday for people not doing what they want to do:

- I haven't got the time.
- There are just too many things to do.
- I'll start on Monday (does something magical happen on Monday that doesn't happen on any other day? If there is I sure would like to know).
- First I want to get through this project then I'll get to that. My kids are driving me crazy.
- My friends won't understand. It just takes too much time. I'm going on vacation and will do it when I get back.
- I can't concentrate. It's just too much work.

And the list goes on and on and on. In the end you never complete what you wanted to do. Why? Because you've developed a habit of rationalizing your way out of getting something done – in short you've bought into your excuses. You now believe your excuses and your reasons for not doing something are valid and thus nothing ever gets done. But more importantly—you've been focusing on the wrong thing and that's why you're not getting motivated.

In many cases the most common excuse or reason is time. People always say they don't have time or they will get to it later or they'll wait until they have more time. But what's the reason for creating that excuse. The truth is that it's often really not about time. Let's face it you have 24 hours in a day, you sleep for 8, leaving 16, you work 8 hours or even 10 hours a day that leaves you with 6 or 8 hours a day. Maybe you spend an hour commuting everyday that brings it down to 5 or 7 hours a day. You cook, eat and relax—does that take 5 or 7 hours everyday? No it doesn't. The truth is that if you just spent even a few minutes to an hour a day working towards your goals you'd achieve them. The first reason is not time—instead it's that you've accepted the excuses.

Now the reason why you create the excuse or rationalize your way out of achieving your goals is because you're focusing on the process and not the result that you ultimately want.

When you focus on the process you'll come up with excuses for not doing what you really want to do. Why? Because the process is time consuming, it requires work, you have to put in the effort, and everybody wants things done immediately – we all want results right away. But does a person who wants to be a marathon athlete start off by running the New York Marathon? No. Instead he or she trains sometimes for years before running in the New York Marathon. Does a professional football player become a professional football player without training and playing at least in high school?

No. Does a successful company generate millions of dollars in profits overnight? No. They all go through a process, which to the average outsider appears to be excruciating and time consuming because they're not involved in the process and not focused on the reward or the result.

Too often I hear people tell me their excuses for not moving forward and achieving their goals and I know the real reason is that they're focusing on the process and not the result. So the first step to getting motivated is to put aside the excuses and look at what you really want and why – this is where you actually focus on the result that you are looking for.

How To Eliminate The Excuses

If you really want to achieve your goals you have to eliminate the excuses – get them out of your system. Unfortunately you can't reach in and just yank them out. Your mind has become comfortable with these excuses and they are now a part of your daily thinking and living. The good news is that you can eliminate them by replacing them and you do this by first deciding what you want and why – or recognizing and focusing on your motivating factor. Don't just think about the motivating factor – think about achieving that result. Think about how it would feel to have what you want and fulfill that motivating factor. Don't think about having a million dollars – think about having the new home that you would buy, think about the financial security that you would have. If you wanted to be in a relationship don't just think about having a boyfriend or a girlfriend – think about how it would feel to spend time with this person, and to share your life and love with this person. Get the idea? Focus on the result that you want – that's your motivating factor.

For example: you may want to meet someone, get married and settle down – now think of why you want to do this (the motivating factor) – and start to feel as though you've already achieved it. Do this every time you think about the little things that you have to do. If you want to be in a relationship and you don't feel like dating because you have to go through the whole process of going out, meeting someone and dealing with possible rejection – then don't think about that process. Instead, focus on the end result that you're after – which is complete fulfillment and the feeling of love and affection in a strong, powerful commitment with a partner who cares deeply about you and your well-being. When you think about that it feels a lot better than when you think about the process of dating. It's the end result that you want– and when you focus on the end result that you want – you'll put aside the excuses. When you put aside the excuses you give your mind and subconscious mind a new set of instructions and together they attract the situations, people and events to help you achieve your goals.

When you focus on the reason for achieving those goals you actually start to enjoy the process because you have a result in mind that you want to accomplish.   Students who work with Creating Power start to focus on the reason and rewards of their goals in the very first week. They then learn to develop a new way of thinking and living so that their subconscious mind creates the opportunities for them to succeed. You can enjoy the same results by working with everything that I've just outlined.

I know some of you may say: "Karim, you don't understand my situation. I really don't have the time – I barely get a moment to breathe, let alone do anything else. How can I make the time when there aren't enough hours in the day." We all get the same amount of time – how we use that time is up to us. If you don't have the time to make the changes or improvements you want in life then you're really saying they're not important enough. But don't just listen to me – take a look for yourself. Write a list of all the things you do everyday and then see which are so important that they can't be put aside for your goals. And keep in mind – that if you don't make the time for those improvements you want – nothing changes. Remember the reason for those goals – remember the outcome that you want, remember the motivating factor – remember why those goals are so important and how achieving them will significantly change your life. Then see if it's important enough to set aside a few minutes.

Also take a look and see if you are constantly focusing on the process or if you're actually keeping the outcome or result of your goals in mind. Try spending a few minutes during the day thinking about how achieving your goals will change your life. Don't think about the little things that have to be done – just think about how achieving your goal would change or improve your life and do this for just a few minutes a day. Then take the first step and keep in mind the reward. If you want to get a job then think about how having that job would change your life and take the first step by doing something – while focusing on how having that job will change your life. When you focus on the reward or the result of your goals – you send a powerful message to your subconscious mind. You give it a clear reason for accomplishing your goal and usually you have a feeling tied to achieving that goal. Now your subconscious mind has direction, reason and believes that this goal is important because there is feeling attached to the thought. Do this everyday and you'll see yourself getting motivated.

Training The Mind And
Directing The Subconscious

The next step involves training the mind – something that is crucial to your success – regardless of how motivated you are. The mind is comfortable where it is and this is what leads to complacency or procrastination. It's not that you personally don't want to achieve your goals – it's just that your mind is not used to focusing and achieving them. So while you may focus on your goals and the rewards – and you may clearly understand the motivating factors – if you're mind is not on the same page – if your mind does not believe that you can achieve your goals – then you won't achieve them.

The mind has to believe that you can achieve your goals otherwise it won't help you find solutions or help you come up with a plan to achieve them. And if the mind isn't sending the right messages to your subconscious mind then it will often feel like you're spinning your wheels or going in the opposite direction.

How do you get the mind to believe that you can achieve your goals? You first start by regularly focusing on what you want and looking at the reasons of why you want to achieve those goals. Then you have to look at why you can in fact achieve them. If you think your goals are too far away or out of reach – then start with small goals. For example: if you want to make a million dollars but you feel it's impossible to do at this precise moment and in a short period of time – then start by focusing on making 10-thousand dollars more than you are currently making and build from there. As you achieve that goal – set another smaller goal – perhaps 20-thousand dollars more and so on until you get to a point where your mind feels comfortable with the idea that you can make a million dollars. If you do this regularly, and you focus on the reason for achieving those goals you'll start to get ideas sooner and you'll get on the track to making a million dollars a lot sooner.

Too often I hear from prospective students who want to change things right away – they want to make that million dollars right now – but their mind won't accept the possibility that they can make a million dollars. You first have to believe that you can do something before you actually do it.

Along the way you have to make the right decisions. And this is where you need to send the right messages to the subconscious mind – because it can guide you and provide the information you need to make that decision. How do you do this? I get into this aspect a lot more in my Creating Power system – but to help you make the right decisions when it comes to the choices you're being presented you should focus on what you want. Don't focus on the choices – focus on making the right choice – that's what you want to do. Tell yourself that you are making the right choice and you will make the right choice. Think about your options regularly, feed your mind and subconscious mind all the information you possibly can and then tell yourself that you are making the right choice. Finally – remember to trust and let go.

Focus on the Positive

The next thing you can do is focus on the positive. I know you've probably heard this before and everybody has probably told you to think positive or be positive. But positive thinking is a practice – it's something you have to do each and everyday so that it becomes a habit. When you have this habit of thinking and focusing on the positive – you attract more positive situations into your life. You can't be positive on occasion – it has to be the norm so that you vibrate positive energy all the time and constantly attract positive situations, people and events. When you do this you begin achieving your goals at a rapid rate.

Achieving this level requires that you understand that there is always a positive situation in everything. Often we don't know what that positive situation is until much later – sometimes even years later.

Here's an example. A good friend of mine, Thomas, broke up with his girlfriend in 2001. At the time he was living in Los Angeles, his family was from New York. Thomas had been engaged and when the relationship ended he was devastated. At the time he saw nothing positive in the situation. Tom had only been living in Los Angeles for her and to top it – he had lost a lot of money when the relationship ended. After talking to him for some time and getting him to work with my Creating Power system, Thomas decided it was time for a change. He moved back to New York to be closer to his family and life-long friends. A year later he met another girl and is now in love again. At the time of writing this they had just been married, bought a new home and were talking about starting a family. When I spoke with Tom just before the wedding he simply said; "Karim, so much has changed and it's all been for the better. 3 years ago I didn't think this was possible – now I know what you meant when you said something good will come out of it. I'm so happy I moved back home – it's the wisest decision I ever made. But it wouldn't have happened had my last relationship not ended." It's funny how things happen and how they change so quickly. But these kinds of changes can only happen when you're open to new possibilities and when you're positive – when you understand and accept that good things can and will happen if you let them – they will happen.

Tom also did another interesting thing that allowed him to enjoy the changes – he moved on from his past relationship by focusing on what he wanted next. He didn't try to win his ex-fiancé back. He didn't focus on meeting another girl right away. He wanted to be happy again, he wanted to enjoy life again and he wanted to live close to his family so that he could experience and share their love and warmth. So he moved back home. His motivating factor was to enjoy life and experience the warmth of his family. In the process – when he was ready, he focused on meeting and being with the right person. I worked with Tom quite a bit during this transition – but he grasped the concepts of Creating Power and what I teach in this book very quickly and was able to accept that change had happened – he could embrace it or fight it. Once he embraced it he was able to decide what he wanted. When he understood his motivating factor – the decisions became easy. You too can enjoy the same level of success by simply applying the principles and techniques that I've outlined here in this book.

I know some of you will say: "Karim, I've been through a lot – and have yet to see anything good come out of all those negative situations." If you sit around and wait for them they won't happen. If you trust that they will happen, stay positive and be open to new possibilities then they will happen. Things would not have improved for my friend had he not been open to the idea of moving back home. Things would not have improved if he didn't accept that something positive would have happened to him in his life.

My friend Tom would not have been motivated to move on with his life if he didn't understand why he wanted a new relationship and why he wanted to settle down.

He had to go through the process – just like you do and during that process you will discover what you want and understand why it is so important – then you will begin to apply the techniques to help you achieve your goals.

Staying motivated is crucial to your success because if you're not motivated to do anything – nothing is going to get done. So let's recap the key things that you need to do in order to stay motivated.

First know what it is you want to achieve and why – the why is your motivating factor. Understand that there are little things that have to be done and when you want to get started – think of your motivating factor, think of the outcome that you want, think of how achieving your goal will change your life – this is your motivating factor.

Second, eliminate the excuses. When you find yourself coming up with excuses – change your thoughts, and shift your focus. Think of why you want to achieve your goals and again start thinking of the motivating factor.

Third – keep training the mind and subconscious mind to focus on your goals so that you take the right steps and continuously move in the direction of achieving your goals and creating the life you want. You do this by regularly thinking about your goals, by regularly looking at different options to achieve them, staying open to new possibilities and taking a look at all of the opportunities you are presented with. To keep your subconscious mind engaged and focus on your goals you need to regularly think about them and regularly encourage yourself to keep taking the right action to help you achieve your goals. Give yourself positive re-enforcement by working with positive statements and looking at the progress you're making everyday. Don't focus on what is wrong – focus on what is right.

These are the key elements to help you stay motivated. Students who work with my Creating Power system work with a number of different techniques to stay motivated, engage and direct their subconscious mind and achieve their goals. You have the basis to get started and if you simply work with the techniques I've outlined you'll stay motivated and you'll increase your chances for success and begin living the life you want.

Here now are some questions from students and subscribers on the issue of staying motivated:

Question:

"Hi Karim,
Every year I set my goals, and I'm filled with excitement. For a couple of weeks I feel like a new person as I set out to achieve my goals. I feel empowered and full of life. But after a few months I seem to lose my drive. I no longer feel as excited and then I seem to give up on my goals and everything goes back to the way it was. I just can't seem to stay motivated. I would appreciate any advice or am I just a hopeless cause?"
-Adina C, Illinois

Answer:

Hi Adina,
What you experience is quite normal – many people start the year feeling empowered as they set out to achieve their goals. You're not a hopeless cause and there is plenty that you can do to stay motivated. One of the reasons why you no longer feel excited is simply because you lost sight and focus of your goals. You stopped thinking about them and you stopped making your goals a priority. Understand that your mind is not used to thinking about your goals, it is not used to looking for ways for you to achieve your goals and thus your subconscious mind is not aware that these

goals are a priority and that you want to achieve them. In order to get your subconscious mind to begin helping you achieve your goals you need to train your mind to regularly work on achieving these goals. Work with the techniques that I've outlined, create affirmations that correspond with achieving your goals and encourage yourself as you make progress and take small steps toward achieving your goals. In the beginning you'll be excited with the process but after a while your mind will want to go back to what it knows – that's only because it's not trained to work on achieving your goals. You have to train your mind to work differently and in the process you'll be instructing your subconscious mind to help you achieve your goals. Finally – remember why your goals are important – this is your motivating factor. Understand why you want to achieve those goals and keep this in mind everyday – make it a habit to work towards your goals everyday by taking action, training your mind and directing your subconscious mind.

Question:

"Karim, I can't believe that some of the most successful people like Bill Gates or Warren Buffet do exercises like those that you outline. Why do we have to do them and they don't?"

Answer:

Hi there,

Some of the most successful people in the world like those that you mentioned automatically think the way that you should. They have been brought up to think in a positive way and focus on what they want. They will also tell you that in order to be successful you have to pay attention to the big picture, be open minded, believe in yourself and work towards achieving your goals. What I have outlined is not something that is taught in schools, maybe it should be – but those who are successful automatically do the things that I have outlined. Why do you have to do them? You don't. But if you have a negative belief system, if you do not believe in yourself, if you cannot stay motivated and if you are not open-minded then I suggest you work with the techniques that I have outlined here and in my Creating Power system. These techniques are proven effective and they will work as long as you work with them regularly.

Question:

"I have a long list of goals – I have achieved not one. I really want to live a better life but I just don't know how to get myself to have the success that I want."

Answer:

It's great that you have goals; my only concern is that you have a long list of goals. Now take a look

the situations you don't want and you will be guided to the people, situations and circumstances that will help you achieve your goals.

For example: if you want to be in a loving, caring, intimate relationship and you've been working with the techniques I've outlined then when a friend invites you to a party it is your responsibility to go with him or her. Because at that party you may meet your partner, you may meet someone else who could introduce you to your partner, you may meet people that could help you decide just what kind of person you want to be with or the kind of person that you don't want to be with. And you may just help someone improve his or her life in some way. Yes it's not always about you – if you've put out a message that you're willing to accept the help of others – then you will also have to help others achieve their goals. If you're not willing to do this then you're best off living on a deserted island. Why? Because we are all connected. If we want others to help us – we have to be willing to help others – we get what we give.

So it's not always all about you – and this is another principle that you will have to accept. If you want to be successful, happy and enjoy the life you want – you're going to have to give the best of yourself in order to receive the best from the world and from others – because you can't get what you don't give. In other words, if you want people to be kind to you – then be kind to others. If you want people to understand you – then be understanding when you're dealing with others. If you want others to help you – then you have to be willing to help others. But here's the catch: You can't do any of the above with the expectation of getting something in return. You have to be good, kind, understanding and nice to others from your heart – you do it because you believe it's the right thing to do and the right way to behave. If you are simply kind, understanding, loving and caring simply because you want something in return – you'll only attract people who are the same and in the end you won't achieve the success and happiness you are looking for. Remember – you'll get what you give. Do things from the heart and you'll attract people who are similar. Do something with the expectation of getting something in return and you'll attract people who will use you in a similar way.

Force yourself to perform at a higher level. Push yourself to be a better person, push yourself to do the exercises that I've outlined and you'll enjoy more success and happiness than you can imagine.

You now know that the basic premise is that your thoughts create your future so keep your thoughts positive. Guard your thoughts, filter them, choose to have positive thoughts and follow up with positive thoughts and actions. Too often people think that they can think wonderful thoughts and carry out terrible actions or say terrible things – expecting their actions and words to have little or no impact. This simply doesn't work and in fact if you have terrific, positive thoughts – but your actions and your words are negative or destructive – the process will actually work against you. Why? Your words are an extension of your thoughts; your actions are also an extension of your thoughts. Everything starts with a thought. In order to do something you have to think it on some level. In order to say something you have to think of the words on some level.

So if you truly want to enjoy success and happiness then it is crucial that you think, act and talk in a way that will attract the situations that you want in your life. If you want to be in a relationship with someone who is caring, loving and thoughtful then in order to attract such a person you would think, and act in a caring, loving and thoughtful way and you would also say things that are caring, loving and thoughtful. You can't expect to be with someone who is caring, loving and thoughtful if you constantly say mean, nasty, inconsiderate things or if you constantly act in a mean, nasty or inconsiderate way.

The next time you're about to get angry, or snap at someone – think about what you want and ask yourself if you would like to be treated the same way as you are about to treat this person? If not – then don't treat them in an unkind way. Treat people with kindness and you'll attract more kindness.

Your actions are a reflection of your thoughts, your words are a reflection of your thoughts and your beliefs are a reflection of your thoughts. So while you may think one thing – if you say or do the opposite of what you think – you neutralize whatever power you were hoping to create.

For example: if you think you're compassionate, but then curse someone when they cut you off while driving, or yell at the postman, or harshly criticize a family member – then you negate any positive energy you hoped to create by thinking you were compassionate. Why? Because your actions, which are a reflection of your thoughts, and your words, which are also a reflection of your thoughts, eliminate the positive energy that you were hoping to create by thinking you were compassionate. But it gets much worse – if you consistently speak and do the opposite of what you think you will eventually create or attract what you do and say. And it still gets worse. Since we're all connected, since others will pick up on your negative vibration – you'll end up attracting those that say and do the same things that you say and do – which will only re-enforce the negative vibration that you are constantly creating. Do you see the vicious cycle that you create and it's a cycle that will get more difficult to break as time goes on because your mind will get used to doing things a certain way. So the sooner you break that cycle the better. And the way to break that cycle is to work with the techniques that I've outlined and to constantly have positive thoughts, display positive actions and say positive words – so that you help people and when you do that – you'll attract people who will help you.

If you want to truly enjoy success and happiness then think positive thoughts, say positive things and act in a positive manner. Be the kind of person that you want to have in your life. If you want compassionate, loving, caring, helpful people in your life then display those characteristics constantly. Say and do compassionate, loving, caring and helpful things, then you'll attract people who display the same qualities that you regularly display. When your thoughts, actions and

words are positive you'll attract positive people into your life.

Your thoughts are energy – the kind of energy picked up by your subconscious mind which then acts on the beliefs and thoughts that you regularly hold. But your thoughts also create a vibration that others pick up. This is what attracts the people, circumstances and events that reflect what you believe, what you think and what you value. So if you have thoughts of anger, resentment, fear, worry, doubt, or any negative thought – you create a negative vibration that others pick up. Now most people are not consciously aware of what they are picking up – they're not aware that they are picking up on your negative vibration. Instead they just know it's something that's telling them to stay away from you or to take advantage of you.

If you hold thoughts of kindness, compassion, love, understanding, confidence, or any positive thoughts and beliefs you create a positive vibration – and thus attract positive people, situations and circumstances.

At some point many of you have picked up on another person's energy – in fact you do it everyday. For example: have you ever been to a party where you met someone and just seemed to get along very well. Sure you may have had some things in common – but you were likely picking up on that person's positive energy. Or have you ever met a friend and asked them what was wrong before they even said a word. Sure you may have noticed their body language – but you also picked up on their energy. You were picking up on their vibration – the same vibration I just mentioned.

Our energy and vibrations connect us all, we may not be aware of it on a conscious level – but on a subconscious level we are always picking up on another person's energy. If you're in a relationship or if you're close to a family member you will more readily pick up on their energy and vibration.

Now here's where the process of being connected creates a bigger impact on your family, your friends, the world and you. If you are mean to someone, then you will attract someone who is mean. You will also make the person you were unkind to a target of someone else's unkindness. He or she will likely focus on the fact that you were mean to them and inadvertently attract somebody else who will be mean to him or her. You in turn will attract another mean or unkind person, and the cycle continues until you consciously decide to break the pattern. This is how what goes around comes around – and it all happens because we are all connected.

Here's an example of a student I worked with who initially refused to accept the fact that we were all connected and that she was attracting all of the negative situations that seemed to pop up in her life. Her name is Lauren, and when I first started working with Lauren she had a lot of attitude. She was always right and it was always somebody else's fault. She would explain how her friends always agreed with her – when she felt it was somebody else's fault – they would agree and that proved she was right. Her attitude wasn't always pleasant – she would snap at people, talk down to them, yell at her kids and it was all necessary, she explained, because she had to put people in their place. I asked her: "Lauren, are you ever nice to people." She simply said: "Oh, I'm nice to them – up to a point – but then I have to put them in their place." So I asked: "And why do they have to be put in their place." Here's what she said: "they start talking back, give me attitude, think they know everything – so I have to put them in their place." I explained that what she saw in people, or the people she continually attracted displayed the same characteristics that she regularly displayed. She believed that people were difficult and always have to be put in their place – so she naturally attracted people who were difficult and had to be put in her place.

Now getting Lauren to simply change and I won't say that she is a sweet, kind, and gentle person today. She still has her edge – but after getting her to work with my Creating Power system she started to see the correlation between what she believed and what was in her life. I asked her to simply try an experiment – and that was to do things in a different way for a month. I only wanted her to display the characteristics that she wanted to see in other people. It meant being kinder, open-minded, tolerant, patient, understanding and smarter. After a month – Lauren started to notice a difference in how people responded to her. She also noticed that some of her friends weren't calling as often – after all they didn't agree with her anymore. This wasn't surprising to me – but what was surprising was Lauren's ability to grasp what she had been doing and change that to create what she wanted. As I said earlier, Lauren still has her edge – but she has a lot more quality people in her life today simply by changing her thoughts, actions and words.

If you truly want to improve the quality of your life then you will need to accept the fact that we are all connected and that your thoughts, actions and words have a large impact on the people around you and the quality of your life. It's not enough to simply think positive thoughts, or to focus on the motivating factor – you have to work with the power of connection. You will connect with those that share your thoughts, energy, actions and words. If you want to make millions of dollars then don't speak of lack. If you want to be in a healthy, loving relationship then don't talk about how bad men or women are. If you want to be more confident then don't shy away from people when they speak to you. You are connected to the person sitting next to you – and they will pick up on your energy. Choose your thoughts, actions and words wisely so that you attract the right situations, people and events into your life on a daily basis.

I've given you a lot of material to work with and I've given you a lot to think about. I suggest you get started right away – set up a routine that you can follow. Do certain exercises in the morning, other exercises in the afternoon, another set in the early evening, and another set at night. Your goal should be to make these exercises a part of your daily life – so that they become a habit and become a part of the way you think, live, and act. When this happens, when you are automatically practicing the exercises and techniques that I've outlined you will start to see dramatic results and improvements in your life.

I wish you all the success in life and I know that if you follow the principles and guidelines that I have outlined in this book you will get results. I also encourage you to consider working with my Creating Power system — you can learn more by visiting www.creatingpower.com *or*
you can call toll free in the US and Canada 800-230-8870. Outside the US and Canada you can call 416-227-9665. If you have any questions or comments please feel free to email me at: info@creatingpower.com

Thank you,

Karim Hajee
Creating Power